In the name of Allah, The Most Gracious and The Most Merciful".

THE DUAS BOOK
from
QURAN & HADITH

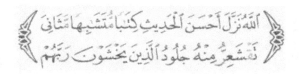

"Allah has revealed the best announcement in
the form of a Book, consistent with itself, repeating
(itst eaching in various aspects): the skins of those who fear their Lord
tremble thereat;"

#		
1.	Introduction	6
2.	Fulfilment Of Religious Needs	7
3.	Death In The State Of Iman	8
4.	Pardon From Allah I	8
5.	Shafa'ah (Intercession Of Rasulullah r)	9
6.	Steadfastness Of The Heart	10
7.	Creating Noor In The Heart	10
8.	Removing Suspicion And Doubt	10
9.	Piety In The Family	11
10.	Protection From The Fire Of Hell	12
11.	Noor On The Face	13
12.	Safety From Punishment In The Grave	14
13.	Awakening In The Night	14
14.	To Simplify The Memorizing Of The Qur'an	17
15.	Maintaining Correct Beliefs	17
16.	Correcting One's Beliefs	17
17.	Pleasure Of Allah I	17
18.	Removing Of A Calamity	17
19.	Assured Acceptance Of Du'a	18
20.	Fulfilment Of Any Need	21
21.	Improving The Memory	21
22.	Removing Fear And Grief	23
23.	Acquiring A Son	23
24.	Virtuous Children	23
25.	Sterility	23

26.	Miscarriage	24
27.	Labour Pains	24
28.	Protecting Children Against Infantile Diseases	25
29.	Healthy Upbringing Of Children	25
30.	For Abundance In Rizq	26
31.	Repayments Of Debts	28
32.	To Please Someone Endowed With Power	29
33.	To Halt An Oppressor From Oppressing	30
34.	Disobedient Children	30
35.	For Insubordination And Disobedience	31
36.	Protection Against Evil Men And Jinn	32
37.	Removing Fear	33
38.	To Remove Fear And Fright	33
39.	Security Against All Harms	34
40.	Curing Someone Under The Influence Of Evil	39
41.	To Drive Out Jinn From A House	40
42.	Imam Auza'i (R.A.) And The Evil Jinn	40
43.	To Overpower One's Opponents In Debate	41
44.	To Overcome A Foe In Any Contest Or Battle	47
45.	Barakah In Produce, Livestock Etc	47
46.	Barakah In Business, Farming, Home Etc	47
47.	To Drive Away Pests	49
48.	For Barakah And Progress In Business	51
49.	For Progress And Protection In Business	52
50.	To Keep Justice	52
51.	For Lessening One's Burden	53
52.	When Entering A Town	54

53.	When Boarding Any Means Of Conveyance/transport	55
54.	Protection Of A Vessel	55
55.	When The Seas Are Rough	57
56.	For Returning Home Safe And Sound	57
57.	Fever	59
58.	For Any Sickness	59
59.	To Remove Pain	61
60.	To Cure Insomnia	61
61.	More Prescriptions For All Types Of Ailments	61
62.	For Melancholy And Depression	63
63.	Palpitation Of The Heart	63
64.	Ailment Of The Heart	63
65.	Strengthening The Heart	64
66.	To Acquire Freedom From Materialism	65
67.	Disease Of The Spleen	66
68.	For A Specific Pain	66
69.	Headaches	67
70.	Migraine	68
71.	Inflammation Of The Eyes	70
72.	Strengthening The Eyesight	72
73.	Pain In The Kidney	73
74.	Epilepsy	74
75.	Paralysis Of The Body	74
76.	Leprosy	75
77.	Itching Of The Body	78
78.	Bone Fracture	79
79.	Forgetfulness	80

80.	To Remove Hardheartedness	81
81.	Barakah In Food	81
82.	The Price Of Jannah	81
83.	Nightmares	81
84.	Insomnia	82
85.	The 99 Beautiful Names Of Allah I	83
86.	For Protection Against Thieves	84
87.	Safeguarding Of Money And Valuables	86
88.	To Find A Lost Object	86
89.	For The Return Of Someone Who Has Absconded	87
	Ensuring The Safety Of One's Family And Property During Ones Absence	87
	Protection Against All Types Of Animals, Insects And Reptiles	88
92.	Protection Against Snakes And Scorpions	89
	To Prevent Dangerous Animals, Harmful Insects And Reptiles From Entering The House	90
94.	When Fearing An Attack From An Animal	90
95.	When Bitten By A Poisonous Insect Or Snake	91
96.	When Stung By An Insect	92
97.	General Protection	92
98.	To Drive Out Ants From The House	92
99.	To Drive Out Mosquitoes, Fleas Etc	93
100.	Release From Imprisonment	93
	Muslim's Invisible Enemies And The Way To Overcome Them:	94

FULFILMENT OF RELIGIOUS NEEDS

A. الٓمٓ ۝ اللّٰهُ لَآ اِلٰهَ اِلَّا هُوَ الْحَىُّ الْقَيُّوْمُ ۝

Alif Laam Meem. Allah!
There is none worthy of worship but He,
The Ever-Living, The Eternal.

Al Imran 1,2

Significance: According to some *Hadith*, The *Ismul-A'zam* is contained in this verse. It is most effective if read continually in times of calamity.

B. لَّآ اِلٰهَ اِلَّآ اَنْتَ سُبْحٰنَكَ اِنِّىْ كُنْتُ مِنَ الظّٰلِمِيْنَ ۝

None is worthy of worship besides You.
You are Pure (and) surely, I am from among the transgressors.

Al Ambiya 87

Significance: The *Ismul-A'zam* is according to other traditions contained in the above verse. A person will profit tremendously if he recites it for any legitimate purpose.

C. هُوَ اللّٰهُ الَّذِىْ لَآ اِلٰهَ اِلَّا هُوَ ۚ عٰلِمُ الْغَيْبِ وَالشَّهَادَةِ ۚ

هُوَ الرَّحْمٰنُ الرَّحِيْمُ ۝

Allah is He besides whom there is none worthy of worship.
He is the Knower of both secret and open.
He is Most Kind, Most Merciful.

Al Hashr 22

Significance: The Ismul-A'zam is, according to some, concealed in the above verse. Anyone who recites it seven times in the morning, an angel will be appointed to seek pardon on his behalf till the evening. If he happens to die on that day, he will die as a martyr. 'And if he reads it seven times in the evening, the angels will seek pardon for him till the morning. If he happens to die during the night, he will die as a martyr.

DEATH IN THE STATE OF IMAN

رَبَّنَا لَا تُزِغْ قُلُوبَنَا بَعْدَ اِذْ هَدَيْتَنَا وَهَبْ لَنَا مِنْ لَّدُنْكَ رَحْمَةً ۚ اِنَّكَ اَنْتَ الْوَهَّابُ ۞

Our Lord! Let not our hearts deviate after You have guided us.
And (instead) grant us Your special mercy, for You are the Granter
of bounties without limits.

Al Imran 8

Significance: Anyone who recites this Du'a' after each Salaah, he shall die in the state of Iman — Insha Allah.

PARDON FROM ALLAH I

رَبَّنَا ظَلَمْنَآ اَنْفُسَنَا ۔ وَاِنْ لَّمْ تَغْفِرْلَنَا وَتَرْحَمْنَا

$$\text{لَنَكُونَنَّ مِنَ الْخَاسِرِينَ ﴿٢٣﴾}$$

Our Lord! We have wronged our souls:
If You do not forgive us and bestow upon us Your mercy, then we shall
certainly be from amongst the losers.

Al A'raf 23

Significance: Anyone who recites this Du'a once after every Fardh Salaah, Allah I will grant him pardon - Insha-Allah. This is the Du'a of Adam u after he was transferred on to the earth.

SHAFA'AH (INTERCESSION OF RASULULLAH r)

$$\text{لَقَدْ جَآءَكُمْ رَسُولٌ مِّنْ أَنْفُسِكُمْ عَزِيزٌ عَلَيْهِ}$$
$$\text{مَا عَنِتُّمْ حَرِيصٌ عَلَيْكُمْ بِالْمُؤْمِنِينَ رَءُوفٌ رَّحِيمٌ ﴿١٢٨﴾}$$
$$\text{فَإِنْ تَوَلَّوْا فَقُلْ حَسْبِيَ اللهُ لَآ إِلٰهَ إِلَّا هُوَ ۖ}$$
$$\text{عَلَيْهِ تَوَكَّلْتُ وَهُوَ رَبُّ الْعَرْشِ الْعَظِيمِ ﴿١٢٩﴾}$$

Surely, an Apostle from amongst you has come unto you:
Your harms grieve him: he is ardently anxious over you: to the Believers he is
mot kind and merciful. But if they turn away,
say: 'Allah suffices me: There is none worthy of worship but He:
upon Him is my trust - He is Lord of the Great Throne.'

At Tawbah 128,129

Significance: Whoever recites these verses once after every Salaah, he will attain the intercession of Rasulullah r on the Day of Judgement - Insha-Allah. Moreover, it is very effective in removing any harm.

STEADFASTNESS OF THE HEART

فَاسْتَقِمْ كَمَآ أُمِرْتَ وَمَنْ تَابَ مَعَكَ

Be firm (upon the Right Path) just as You had been commanded and those who had repented with You, (had been commanded).

Hud 112

Significance: For steadfastness of the heart, recite 11 times after every Salaah.

CREATING NOOR IN THE HEART

A. SURAH AL KAHF

Significance: Whoever recites Surah Al Kahf once every Friday, his heart will remain filled with noor till the following Friday. Whoever recites the first 10 verses of this Surah every day, he will be safeguarded against the fitnah of Dajjal.

REMOVING SUSPICION AND DOUBT

رَّبِّ أَعُوذُ بِكَ مِنْ هَمَزَاتِ الشَّيَاطِينِ ۝

وَأَعُوذُ بِكَ رَبِّ أَنْ يَحْضُرُونِ ۝

My Lord! I seek your protection from the prompting of the Devils; and my Lord! I seek your protection from them approaching me.

Al Muminun 97, 98

Significance: The excessive recitation of the above verses removes all suspicion and doubt.

PIETY IN THE FAMILY

رَبَّنَا هَبْ لَنَا مِنْ اَزْوَاجِنَا وَذُرِّيّٰتِنَا قُرَّةَ اَعْيُنٍ وَّاجْعَلْنَا لِلْمُتَّقِيْنَ اِمَامًا ۝

Our Lord, let our wives and offspring be a means of the coolness of our eyes and make us the leaders of the righteous people.

Al Furqan 74

Significance: Anyone desirous of righteous children and a righteous wife should recite the above verse once after each Salaah.

PROTECTION FROM THE FIRE OF HELL

حٰمٓ ۚ تَنْزِيْلُ الْكِتٰبِ مِنَ اللهِ الْعَزِيْزِ الْعَلِيْمِ ۙ

حٰمٓ ۚ تَنْزِيْلٌ مِّنَ الرَّحْمٰنِ الرَّحِيْمِ ۚ

حٰمٓ ۚ عٓسٓقٓ ۚ

حٰمٓ ۚ وَالْكِتٰبِ الْمُبِيْنِ ۙ

حٰمٓ ۚ وَالْكِتٰبِ الْمُبِيْنِ ۙ

اِنَّآ اَنْزَلْنٰهُ فِيْ لَيْلَةٍ مُّبٰرَكَةٍ اِنَّا كُنَّا مُنْذِرِيْنَ ۚ

حٰمٓ ۚ تَنْزِيْلُ الْكِتٰبِ مِنَ اللهِ الْعَزِيْزِ الْحَكِيْمِ ۙ

حٰمٓ ۚ تَنْزِيْلُ الْكِتٰبِ مِنَ اللهِ الْعَزِيْزِ الْحَكِيْمِ ۙ

Ha. Mim. This Heavenly Book is sent down from Allah, the Almighty, the All-Knowing-

Ha. Mim. This Quran has been sent down from Allah, the Most-Kind, the Ever-Merciful.

Ha. Mim. Ain. Sin. Qaf.

Ha. Mim. By the Book luminous!

Ha. Mim. By the Luminous Book that makes plain the Truth- Surely We have sent it down during a blessed night-truly it is for Us to give timely warning (against evil).

Ha. Mim. This Heavenly Book has been sent down from Allah, the Almighty, the All-Wise.

Ha. Mim. This Heavenly Book is sent down from Allah, the Almighty, the All-Wise.

Significance: *Anyone who recites the above seven Ha Mims constantly, the door of Hell-fire will always remain closed for him, but a person should rather try to recite as much of the Qur'an as possible.*

NOOR ON THE FACE

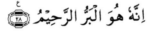

Truly, it is He who is Beneficent, Merciful.

At Tur 28

Significance: *Anyone who recites the above verse 11 times, his face will shine brightly on the Day of Qiyamah ... Insha-Allah.*

SAFETY FROM PUNISHMENT IN THE GRAVE

Significance: *Anyone who recites Surah Al-Mulk daily will be safeguarded against the punishment of the grave.*

AWAKENING IN THE NIGHT

A. وَاِذْ جَعَلْنَا الْبَيْتَ مَثَابَةً لِّلنَّاسِ وَاَمْنًا ۫ وَاتَّخِذُوْا مِنْ مَّقَامِ اِبْرٰهِمَ مُصَلًّى ۫ وَعَهِدْنَآ اِلٰۤى اِبْرٰهِمَ وَاِسْمٰعِيْلَ اَنْ طَهِّرَا بَيْتِىَ لِلطَّآئِفِيْنَ وَالْعٰكِفِيْنَ وَالرُّكَّعِ السُّجُوْدِ ۞

And remember the time when We made The House a place of worship for the people and a place of safety.
And take the Maqam Ibrahim as a place of performing Salaah.
And We decreed to Ibrahim and Isma'il that they should purify My House for those who observe Tawaaf of it and those who observe Ruku and those who observe Sajdah (in prayers)

Al Baqarah 125

Significance: *It was found written by a certain sage, that anyone who recites the above verse before retiring to bed, he will be able to get up at any time he desires.*

B. اِنَّ فِیْ خَلْقِ السَّمٰوٰتِ وَالْاَرْضِ وَاخْتِلَافِ الَّیْلِ وَالنَّهَارِ لَاٰیٰتٍ لِّاُولِی الْاَلْبَابِ ۚ۝ الَّذِیْنَ یَذْکُرُوْنَ اللّٰہَ قِیَامًا وَّقُعُوْدًا وَّعَلٰی جُنُوْبِہِمْ وَیَتَفَکَّرُوْنَ فِیْ خَلْقِ السَّمٰوٰتِ وَالْاَرْضِ ۚ رَبَّنَا مَا خَلَقْتَ ہٰذَا بَاطِلًا ۚ سُبْحٰنَکَ فَقِنَا عَذَابَ النَّارِ ۝

رَبَّنَاۤ اِنَّکَ مَنْ تُدْخِلِ النَّارَ فَقَدْ اَخْزَیْتَہٗ ؕ وَمَا لِلظّٰلِمِیْنَ مِنْ اَنْصَارٍ ۝ رَبَّنَاۤ اِنَّنَا سَمِعْنَا مُنَادِیًا یُّنَادِیْ لِلْاِیْمَانِ اَنْ اٰمِنُوْا بِرَبِّکُمْ فَاٰمَنَّا ۚ رَبَّنَا فَاغْفِرْ لَنَا ذُنُوْبَنَا وَکَفِّرْ عَنَّا سَیِّاٰتِنَا وَتَوَفَّنَا مَعَ الْاَبْرَارِ ۝ رَبَّنَا وَ اٰتِنَا مَا وَعَدْتَّنَا عَلٰی رُسُلِکَ وَلَا تُخْزِنَا یَوْمَ الْقِیٰمَۃِ ؕ اِنَّکَ لَا تُخْلِفُ الْمِیْعَادَ ۝

Verily in the creation of the heavens and the earth, and in the
alternation of night and day
there are (mighty) signs for men of understanding.
Those men of understanding who remember Allah standing and sitting and
lying on their sides, and keep reflecting on the
wonders of the creation of the heavens and the earth (and admit saying): "Our
Lord! You have not created all this (Universe) in vain.
Glory be to You! Save us Lord!
from the torment of the Blazing Fire.
"Our Lord! whomsoever You cause to enter Hell, him You have surely
disgraced, and for the wrongdoers there shall be no helpers.
"Our Lord! we have heard a proclaimer calling to Faith (saying):
'Believe in your Lord;' so we have come to believe.
Our Lord! forgive us our sins, and wipe off our misdeeds from us and cause us (in
all grace) to die with the righteous.
"Our Lord! grant us that which You have promised to us through Your Apostles
and disgrace us not on the Day of Reckoning.
Surely You never fail in your Promise."

Al Imran 190,194

Significance: Anyone who recites the first 5 verses of the last Ruku of Surah Al-Imran before going to bed, his Iman will remain intact and he will be able to wake up at any time he desires without any assistance whatsoever.

TO SIMPLIFY THE MEMORIZING OF THE QUR'AN

Significance: Recite Surah Muddath-thir, then make Du'a. Insha-Allah memorising the Qur'an will become easy.

MAINTAINING CORRECT BELIEFS

Significance: Excessive recitation of Surah Al-Ikhlaas will enable a person to adopt and maintain correct beliefs and safeguard himself against shirk.

CORRECTING ONE'S BELIEFS

Significance: Recite Surah Al-Ikhaas morning and evening. It is very effective in safeguarding one's Iman and beliefs.

PLEASURE OF ALLAH I

اَلْعَفُوُّ

Significance: To have one's sins atoned and to gain the pleasure of the Almighty, recite the above name of Allah I excessively.

REMOVING OF A CALAMITY

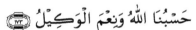

Allah suffices for us and He is the Best Disposer of affairs. Al Imran 173

Significance: Continuous recitation of the above verse is very effective in removing all difficulties and calamities.

ASSURED ACCEPTANCE OF DUA

اِنَّ فِیْ خَلْقِ السَّمٰوٰتِ وَالْاَرْضِ وَاخْتِلَافِ الَّیْلِ وَالنَّهَارِ لَاٰیٰتٍ لِّاُولِی الْاَلْبَابِ ۞ الَّذِیْنَ یَذْکُرُوْنَ اللهَ قِیٰمًا وَّقُعُوْدًا وَّعَلٰی جُنُوْبِهِمْ وَیَتَفَکَّرُوْنَ فِیْ خَلْقِ السَّمٰوٰتِ وَالْاَرْضِ ۚ رَبَّنَا مَا خَلَقْتَ هٰذَا بٰطِلًا ۚ سُبْحٰنَکَ فَقِنَا عَذَابَ النَّارِ ۞ رَبَّنَآ اِنَّکَ مَنْ تُدْخِلِ النَّارَ فَقَدْ اَخْزَیْتَهٗ ؕ وَمَا لِلظّٰلِمِیْنَ مِنْ اَنْصَارٍ ۞ رَبَّنَآ اِنَّنَا سَمِعْنَا مُنَادِیًا یُّنَادِیْ لِلْاِیْمَانِ اَنْ اٰمِنُوْا بِرَبِّکُمْ فَاٰمَنَّا ۖ رَبَّنَا فَاغْفِرْ لَنَا ذُنُوْبَنَا وَکَفِّرْ عَنَّا سَیِّاٰتِنَا وَتَوَفَّنَا مَعَ الْاَبْرَارِ ۞ رَبَّنَا وَ اٰتِنَا مَا وَعَدْتَّنَا عَلٰی رُسُلِکَ وَلَا تُخْزِنَا یَوْمَ الْقِیٰمَةِ ؕ اِنَّکَ لَا تُخْلِفُ الْمِیْعَادَ ۞

For Translation See Awaking at Night on page 14

Significance: Rasulullah r used to recite the above verses after Tahajjud Salaah. The fact that Rasulullah r used to recite them after Tahajjud is sufficient proof as to the assured acceptance of the Du'a that appear in them. Any Du'a made after their recital will also be accepted by Allah I — Insha-Allah.

B. فَقُلْتُ اسْتَغْفِرُوْا رَبَّكُمْ ۖ اِنَّهٗ كَانَ غَفَّارًا ۝ يُّرْسِلِ السَّمَآءَ عَلَيْكُمْ مِّدْرَارًا ۝ وَّيُمْدِدْكُمْ بِاَمْوَالٍ وَّبَنِيْنَ وَيَجْعَلْ لَّكُمْ جَنّٰتٍ وَّيَجْعَلْ لَّكُمْ اَنْهٰرًا ۝

And I said: Ask forgiveness from your Lord for He is Oft-Forgiving
He will send rain to you in abundance,
He will give you increase in wealth and sons and bestow on you
gardens and bestow on you rivers.

Nuh 10,12

Significance: Du'a are certainly accepted after Istighfar as understood from the above.

C. اَللّٰهُ لَآ اِلٰهَ اِلَّا هُوَ ۚ اَلْحَىُّ الْقَيُّوْمُ ەۚ لَا تَأْخُذُهٗ سِنَةٌ وَّلَا نَوْمٌ ۖ لَهٗ مَا فِي السَّمٰوٰتِ وَمَا فِي الْاَرْضِ ۗ مَنْ ذَا الَّذِىْ يَشْفَعُ عِنْدَهٗٓ

اِلَّا بِاِذْنِهٖ ۚ يَعْلَمُ مَا بَيْنَ اَيْدِيْهِمْ وَمَا خَلْفَهُمْ ۚ وَلَا يُحِيْطُوْنَ بِشَيْءٍ مِّنْ عِلْمِهٖٓ اِلَّا بِمَا شَآءَ ۚ وَسِعَ كُرْسِيُّهُ السَّمٰوٰتِ وَالْاَرْضَ ۚ وَلَا يَـُٔوْدُهٗ حِفْظُهُمَا ۚ وَهُوَ الْعَلِيُّ الْعَظِيْمُ ۞

Allah, none is worthy of worship except He, the Hayyul Qayyoom (the ever-living, the One who sustains and protects all that exists). Neither slumber nor sleep overtakes Him.
To Him belongs whatever is in the heavens and earth.
Who is there that can intercede before Him except by His permission?
He knows what happens to them before them and behind them. And they will never encompass anything of His knowledge except that which He wills.
His throne extends over the heavens and earth.
And He feels no fatigue in guarding them.
And He is Most High, Most Great.

Al Baqarah 255

Significance: Recite Aayatul-Kursi 70 times after Asr Salaah on Friday. Sit in seclusion while doing this. A special and marvelous feeling will be experienced in the heart. Any Du'a made after this, will be assuredly accepted by Allah I — Insha-Allah.

D. اَلْمُجِيْبُ

The One who Responds.

Significance: *For the assured acceptance of Du'a call upon Allah I by His above attribute numerous times while making Du'a.*

FULFILMENT OF ANY NEED

فَاِنْ تَوَلَّوْا فَقُلْ حَسْبِیَ اللّٰهُ ۖ لَاۤ اِلٰهَ اِلَّا هُوَ ؕ عَلَیْهِ تَوَكَّلْتُ وَهُوَ رَبُّ الْعَرْشِ الْعَظِیْمِ ۞

But if they away, say: Allah suffices me. None is worthy of worship but He.
On Him is my trust and He is the Lord of the Supreme Throne.

At Tawbah 129

Significance: *Abu Darda t relates that any person who recites the above ayah 100 times, all his worldly needs and his needs pertaining to the Hereafter will be fulfilled.*

IMPROVING THE MEMORY

رَبِّ اشْرَحْ لِیْ صَدْرِیْ ۞ وَیَسِّرْ لِیْ اَمْرِیْ ۞
وَاحْلُلْ عُقْدَةً مِّنْ لِّسَانِیْ ۞ یَفْقَهُوْا قَوْلِیْ ۞

My Lord! Expand for me my bosom.
Ease my task for me.
Remove the knot from my speech so that they may understand what I say.

Ta-Ha 25,28

Significance: For strengthening the memory and progressing in knowledge recite the above verses every day after Fardh Salaah.

REMOVING FEAR AND GRIEF

Significance: The recitation of Surah Nooh is very effective in removing grief and fear. Also Surah Yasin is most effective in removing all types of fear — especially for one's life. It is reported from Ibnul-Kalbi that a certain person's life had been threatened. He reported the matter to an alim who advised him to recite Surah Yasin every time he leaves his home. He did exactly as he was told with the result that every time he came before his enemy, the latter failed to see him.

ACQUIRING A SON

رَبِّ هَبْ لِيْ مِنْ لَّدُنْكَ ذُرِّيَّةً طَيِّبَةً

اِنَّكَ سَمِيْعُ الدُّعَآءِ ۝

O My Lord! Grant me from Yourself a progeny that is pure: for You are the Granter of prayers.

Al Imran 38

Significance: By the excessive recitation of the above verse, a person will acquire a virtuous and righteous son. — Insha Allah.

VIRTUOUS CHILDREN

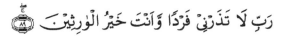

Significance: Recite the above ayah three times after every Salaah. Good and righteous children will be granted — Insha Allah.

STERILITY

اَلْبَارِئُ الْمُصَوِّرُ

The Shaper out of naught, The Fashioner.

Significance: *If a barren woman fasts for seven days and after breaking her fast with water, (she should eat food thereafter) reads the above Name of Allah I 21 times then she will soon conceive — Insha Allah.*

MISCARRIAGE

اَللّٰهُ يَعْلَمُ مَا تَحْمِلُ كُلُّ اُنْثٰى وَمَا تَغِيْضُ الْاَرْحَامُ وَمَا تَزْدَادُ ۚ وَكُلُّ شَيْءٍ عِنْدَهٗ بِمِقْدَارٍ ۞

Allah knows that which every female bears and that which the wombs absorb and that which they grow.
And everything with Him is measured.

Ar Ra'd 8

Significance: *If there is fear of miscarriage the above verse should be recited.*

LABOUR PAINS

اَوَلَمْ يَرَ الَّذِيْنَ كَفَرُوْٓا اَنَّ السَّمٰوٰتِ وَالْاَرْضَ كَانَتَا رَتْقًا فَفَتَقْنٰهُمَا ۚ وَجَعَلْنَا مِنَ الْمَآءِ كُلَّ شَيْءٍ حَيٍّ ۚ اَفَلَا يُؤْمِنُوْنَ ۞

Have not those who disbelieve known that the heavens and the earth were of one piece,
then We parted them, and We made every living thing of water? Will they not then believe?

Al Ambiya 30

Significance: When a woman is in the throes of labour, the above verse should be recited by someone (female or mahram male) and then blown on the stomach or back of the woman.

PROTECTING CHILDREN AGAINST INFANTILE DISEASES

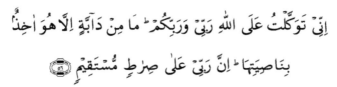

Lo! have put my trust in Allah, My Lord and your Lord.
There is not an animal but He (Allah) grasps it by its forelock! Lo! My Lord is on the Straight Path.

Hud 56

Significance: To protect a child from such sicknesses which normally afflict children, the above ayah should be recited and blown on the child.

HEALTHY UPBRINGING OF CHILDREN

الَّذِیْۤ اَحْسَنَ كُلَّ شَیْءٍ خَلَقَهٗ وَبَدَاَ خَلْقَ الْاِنْسَانِ مِنْ

$$طِينٍ ۝ ثُمَّ جَعَلَ نَسْلَهُ مِنْ سُلَالَةٍ مِنْ مَاءٍ مَهِينٍ ۝$$

$$ثُمَّ سَوَّاهُ وَنَفَخَ فِيهِ مِنْ رُوحِهِ وَجَعَلَ لَكُمُ السَّمْعَ$$

$$وَالْأَبْصَارَ وَالْأَفْئِدَةَ ۚ قَلِيلًا مَا تَشْكُرُونَ ۝$$

He Who made everything par excellence which He created, and He began the creation of man from clay.
Then He created his progeny from an extract of mean water.
Then He set him aright in form and feature and breathed into him of His Spirit, and He gave you ears, eyes and hearts.
But you give little thanks (for these gifts).

As Sajdah 7

Significance: The above verses should be recited and du'a should be made.

FOR ABUNDANCE IN RIZQ

$$اَللّٰهُ لَطِيفٌ بِعِبَادِهِ يَرْزُقُ مَنْ يَشَاءُ$$

$$وَهُوَ الْقَوِيُّ الْعَزِيزُ ۝$$

Allah is gracious unto His slaves
He provides for whom He wills.
And He is the Strong, the Mighty.

As Shura 19

Significance: *For increment in one's rizq, recite the above ayah excessively after each Salaah.*

B. وَمَنْ يَّتَوَكَّلْ عَلَى اللهِ فَهُوَ حَسْبُهٗ ؕ اِنَّ اللّٰهَ بٰلِغُ اَمْرِهٖ ؕ

قَدْ جَعَلَ اللّٰهُ لِكُلِّ شَيْءٍ قَدْرًا ۝

And whoever puts his trust in Allah, He will suffice him.
Lo! Allah brings His commands to pass.
Allah has set a measure for all things.

At Talaq 3

Significance: *Excessive recitation of the above ayah is very effective in removing poverty. If it is recited for any purpose, it will be realised — Insha Allah.*

C. Surah Al Qalam

Significance: Recitation of Surah Al-Qalam in Salaah removes poverty.

D. Surah Al Qari'ah

Significance: Excessive recitation of Surah Al-Qari'ah is very effective in increasing one's rizq.

REPAYMENT OF DEBTS

قُلِ اللّٰهُمَّ مٰلِكَ الْمُلْكِ تُؤْتِي الْمُلْكَ مَنْ تَشَآءُ وَتَنْزِعُ الْمُلْكَ مِمَّنْ تَشَآءُ ؕ وَتُعِزُّ مَنْ تَشَآءُ وَتُذِلُّ مَنْ تَشَآءُ ؕ بِيَدِكَ الْخَيْرُ ؕ اِنَّكَ عَلٰى كُلِّ شَىْءٍ قَدِيْرٌ ۝

Say: O Allah! Master of the sovereignty!
You give sovereignty to whomever You desire, and withdraw
sovereignty from whomever You desire.
You exalt whomever You desire and debase whomever You desire.
In Your hand is goodness.
Truly, You possess power over everything.

Al Imran 26

Significance: Recite the above verse seven times after Fajr and seven times after Maghrib. Insha Allah, Allah I will make means for debts to be settled.

TO PLEASE SOMEONE ENDOWED WITH POWER

A.

كَمْ اٰتَيْنٰهُمْ مِّنْ اٰيَةٍۭ بَيِّنَةٍ ۭ وَمَنْ يُّبَدِّلْ نِعْمَةَ اللّٰهِ مِنْۢ بَعْدِ مَا جَآءَتْهُ فَاِنَّ اللّٰهَ شَدِيْدُ الْعِقَابِ ﴿٢١١﴾

How many a clear revelation we bestowed upon them. He who after the grace of Allah after it been granted to him, Allah will punish him. Lo! Allah is severe in punishment.

Al Baqarah 211

Significance: Recite the following verse thrice and then blow on yourself. After doing this go before the person endowed with power (such as a chief, judge etc.) Insha Allah he will display much sympathy and leniency.

سُبْحٰنَ اللّٰهِ وَتَعٰلٰى عَمَّا يُشْرِكُوْنَ ﴿٦٨﴾ وَرَبُّكَ يَعْلَمُ مَا تُكِنُّ صُدُوْرُهُمْ وَمَا يُعْلِنُوْنَ ﴿٦٩﴾ وَهُوَ اللّٰهُ لَآ اِلٰهَ اِلَّا هُوَ ۭ لَهُ الْحَمْدُ فِى الْاُوْلٰى وَالْاٰخِرَةِ ۭ وَلَهُ الْحُكْمُ وَاِلَيْهِ تُرْجَعُوْنَ ﴿٧٠﴾

Glorified be Allah and exalted above all they associate (with Him).
And Your Lord know what their breasts conceal and what they publish.
And He is Allah. There is no God save Him.
For Him is all praise in the former and latter (state).
For Him is command and unto Him you will be returned.   Al Qasas 68,70

Significance: *The above ayaat should be recited seven times when there is fear that one's opponent will give false evidence before a judge provoking him to carry out judgement wrongfully. After reciting them seven times, the following verse should be recited thrice before appearing in front of the judge. Insha Allah the reciter will be safeguarded from all forms of evil.*

TO HALT AN OPPRESSOR FROM OPPRESSING

A.

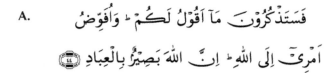

And you will remember what I say unto you.
I confide my cause unto Allah.
Lo! Allah is ever watchful over his slaves.

Al Mumin 44

Significance: *Reciting the above ayah in the presence of the oppressor will safeguard the reciter from his oppression.*

DISOBEDIENT CHILDREN

*And (O Allah), be gracious towards me in the matter of my off-
spring.
And surely, I have returned to You in repentance, and surely, I am of
those who surrender (to You).*

Al Ahqaf 15

Significance: Anyone whose children are disobedient should recite the above Du'a after every Salaah. Insha Allah they will soon become obedient. But have in mind one's children when saying the word Dhurriyyati.

FOR INSUBORDINATION AND DISOBEDIENCE

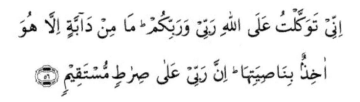

*Lo! I have put my trust in Allah
who is my Lord and your Lord.
There is no animal but He grasp it by its forelock.
Verily my Lord is on the straight path.*

Hud 56

***Significance**: If a person is guilty of insubordination, his/her forelock should be grasped and the above ayah be recited 3 times. Thereafter he/she should be "blown" on. By doing this, Insha Allah, he/she will become obedient, as in accordance to Shariah.*

PROTECTION AGAINST EVIL MEN AND JINN

A. اَللّٰهُ لَاۤ اِلٰهَ اِلَّا هُوَ ۚ اَلْحَىُّ الْقَيُّوْمُ ۚ لَا تَاْخُذُهٗ سِنَةٌ وَّلَا نَوْمٌ ۚ لَهٗ مَا فِى السَّمٰوٰتِ وَمَا فِى الْاَرْضِ ۗ مَنْ ذَا الَّذِىْ يَشْفَعُ عِنْدَهٗۤ اِلَّا بِاِذْنِهٖ ۚ يَعْلَمُ مَا بَيْنَ اَيْدِيْهِمْ وَمَا خَلْفَهُمْ ۚ وَلَا يُحِيْطُوْنَ بِشَىْءٍ مِّنْ عِلْمِهٖۤ اِلَّا بِمَا شَآءَ ۚ وَسِعَ كُرْسِيُّهُ السَّمٰوٰتِ وَالْاَرْضَ ۚ وَلَا يَـُٔوْدُهٗ حِفْظُهُمَا ۚ وَهُوَ الْعَلِىُّ الْعَظِيْمُ ۝

*Allah, none is worthy of worship except He, the Hayyul Qayyoom
(the ever-living, the One who sustains and protects all that exists).
Neither slumber nor sleep overtakes Him.
To Him belongs whatever is in the heavens and earth.
Who is there that can intercede before Him except by His permission?
He knows what happens to them before them and behind them. And they will
never encompass anything of His knowledge except that which He wills.
His throne extends over the heavens and earth.
And He feels no fatigue in guarding them.
And He is Most High, Most Great.*

Al Baqarah 255

Significance: Recitation of the ayatul Kursi once after every Salaah will cause Allah I to protect the reciter against the mischief of evil men and jinn. In fact, according to one Hadith, the Shaytan acknowledged his inability to harm anyone who recites Aayatul Kursi.

B. Surah Al-Falaq And Surah An-Nas

Significance: The last 2 Surah of the Holy Qur'an. To be recited for protection against sicknesses, sorcery, etc. Reciting them before going to bed will afford the reciter security against all calamities.

C. Surah Al-Ikhlas

Significance: Help through the constant recital of Suratul Ikhlaas, the 3rd last Surah of the Holy Qur'an should be sought for any calamity.

REMOVING FEAR

And Allah is the best of Protectors and He is the Most Merciful of all who show Mercy.

Yusuf 64

Significance: One who is terrified of his enemy or fears the approach of any calamity should recite the above verse excessively. Insha Allah his fears will disappear and any possible calamity will be averted.

TO REMOVE FEAR AND FRIGHT

وَاِذَا قَرَاْتَ الْقُرْاٰنَ جَعَلْنَا بَيْنَكَ وَبَيْنَ الَّذِيْنَ لَا يُؤْمِنُوْنَ بِالْاٰخِرَةِ حِجَابًا مَّسْتُوْرًا ۞ وَّجَعَلْنَا عَلٰى قُلُوْبِهِمْ اَكِنَّةً اَنْ

$$\text{يَفْقَهُوهُ وَفِىٓ اٰذَانِهِمْ وَقْرًا ۖ وَاِذَا ذَكَرْتَ رَبَّكَ فِى الْقُرْاٰنِ وَحْدَهٗ وَلَّوْا عَلٰٓى اَدْبَارِهِمْ نُفُوْرًا ۝}$$

And (O My Apostle!) when you recite the Quran,
We set up (to intervene) between you and those who believe not in the Hereafter a hidden
veil invisible to the eye And We put coverings on their hearts that they may not understand it,
and (cause) a heaviness in their ears.
And when you mention your Lord alone in the Quran, they flee away turning on their back in aversion (from the Truth)

Bani Israil 45,46

Significance: The above verses should be recited and blown on any person who is frightened, shocked or terrified. These verses are very effective in removing horrifying thoughts as well.

SECURITY AGAINST ALL HARMS

A. $$\text{اَللّٰهُ رَبُّنَا وَرَبُّكُمْ ۖ لَنَآ اَعْمَالُنَا وَلَكُمْ اَعْمَالُكُمْ ۖ لَا حُجَّةَ بَيْنَنَا وَبَيْنَكُمْ ۖ اَللّٰهُ يَجْمَعُ بَيْنَنَا ۚ}$$

Allah is our Lord and your Lord.
For us is our works and for you is your works.
There are no arguments between us and you. Allah will bring us together.
Ash Shura 15

Significance: *When one fears any injury from any person or animal, the above verse should be recited and "blown" in the direction of such a person or animal. Insha Allah, the person doing this will be protected against any injury.*

B. قُلْ لَّنْ يُّصِيْبَنَآ اِلَّا مَا كَتَبَ اللّٰهُ لَنَا ۚ هُوَ مَوْلٰىنَا ۚ وَعَلَى اللّٰهِ فَلْيَتَوَكَّلِ الْمُؤْمِنُوْنَ ۞

Say: "Nothing shall ever happen to us except what Allah has ordained for us. He is our Maula (Lord, Helper and Protector)." And in Allah let the believers put their trust.

At-Tauba 51

وَاِنْ يَّمْسَسْكَ اللّٰهُ بِضُرٍّ فَلَا كَاشِفَ لَهٗ اِلَّا هُوَ ۚ وَاِنْ يُّرِدْكَ بِخَيْرٍ فَلَا رَآدَّ لِفَضْلِهٖ ۚ يُصِيْبُ بِهٖ مَنْ يَّشَآءُ مِنْ عِبَادِهٖ ۚ وَهُوَ الْغَفُوْرُ الرَّحِيْمُ ۞

And if Allah touches you with hurt, there is none who can remove it but
He, and if He intends any good for you, there is none who can repel His
Favour which He causes it to reach whomsoever of His slaves He wills.
And He is the Oft-Forgiving, the Most Merciful.

Yunus 107

وَمَا مِنْ دَآبَّةٍ فِي الْاَرْضِ اِلَّا عَلَى اللهِ رِزْقُهَا وَيَعْلَمُ مُسْتَقَرَّهَا وَمُسْتَوْدَعَهَا ۚ كُلٌّ فِيْ كِتٰبٍ مُّبِيْنٍ ۝

And no moving (living) creatures is there on earth but its
provision is due from Allah. And He knows its dwelling place and its
deposit
(in the uterus, grave). All is in a Clear Book
(Al-Lauh Al-Mahfuz - the Book of Decrees with Allah).

Hud 6

اِنِّيْ تَوَكَّلْتُ عَلَى اللهِ رَبِّيْ وَرَبِّكُمْ ۭ مَا مِنْ دَآبَّةٍ اِلَّا هُوَ اٰخِذٌۢ بِنَاصِيَتِهَا ۭ اِنَّ رَبِّيْ عَلٰى صِرَاطٍ مُّسْتَقِيْمٍ ۝

*"I put my trust in Allah, my Lord and your Lord!
There is not a moving (living) creature but He has grasp of its forelock. Verily, my
Lord is on the Straight Path (the truth).*

Hud 56

وَكَأَيِّنْ مِّنْ دَآبَّةٍ لَّا تَحْمِلُ رِزْقَهَا ۖ اللّٰهُ يَرْزُقُهَا وَإِيَّاكُمْ ۚ وَهُوَ السَّمِيْعُ الْعَلِيْمُ ۝

And so many a moving (living) creature carries not its own provision! Allah provides for it and for you. And He is the All-Hearer, the All-Knower.

Al-'Ankabut 60

مَا يَفْتَحِ اللّٰهُ لِلنَّاسِ مِنْ رَّحْمَةٍ فَلَا مُمْسِكَ لَهَا ۚ وَمَا يُمْسِكْ فَلَا مُرْسِلَ لَهٗ مِنْۢ بَعْدِهٖ ۚ وَهُوَ الْعَزِيْزُ الْحَكِيْمُ ۝

*Whatever of mercy (i.e. of good),
Allah may grant to mankind, none can withhold it;
and whatever He may withhol, none can grant it thereafter. And He is the All-Mighty, the All-Wise.*

Fatir 2

وَلَئِنْ سَاَلْتَهُمْ مَّنْ خَلَقَ السَّمٰوٰتِ وَالْاَرْضَ لَيَقُوْلُنَّ اللّٰهُ ۭ قُلْ اَفَرَءَيْتُمْ مَّا تَدْعُوْنَ مِنْ دُوْنِ اللّٰهِ اِنْ اَرَادَنِيَ اللّٰهُ بِضُرٍّ هَلْ هُنَّ كٰشِفٰتُ ضُرِّهٖٓ اَوْ اَرَادَنِيْ بِرَحْمَةٍ هَلْ هُنَّ مُمْسِكٰتُ رَحْمَتِهٖ ۭ قُلْ حَسْبِيَ اللّٰهُ ۭعَلَيْهِ يَتَوَكَّلُ الْمُتَوَكِّلُوْنَ ﴿٣٨﴾

*And verily, if you ask them:
"Who created the heavens and the earth?"
Surely, they will say: "Allah (has created them)."
Say: "Tell me them, the things that you invoke besides Allah – if Allah intended some harm for me, could they remove His harm?
Or is He (Allah) intended some mercy for me, could they withhold His Mercy? Say:
"Sufficient for me is Allah; in Him those who trust (i.e. believers) must put their trust."*

Az-Zumar 38

Significance: Ka'ab bin Ahbar t is reported to have said that any person who recites the following seven verses everyday will have no reason to fear any type of harm, whatsoever.

C. Surah Yasin

Significance: It is reported from Ibnul-Kalbi R.A. That a man whose life had been threatened consulted an Alim who advised him to recite Surah Yasin prior to leaving his home. He did just as he was told. The result was that his enemy failed to even notice him.

CURING SOMEONE UNDER THE INFLUENCE OF EVIL

A.

اَفَحَسِبْتُمْ اَنَّمَا خَلَقْنٰكُمْ عَبَثًا وَّاَنَّكُمْ اِلَيْنَا لَا تُرْجَعُوْنَ ۝ فَتَعٰلَى اللهُ الْمَلِكُ الْحَقُّ ۚ لَآ اِلٰهَ اِلَّا هُوَ ۚ رَبُّ الْعَرْشِ الْكَرِيْمِ ۝ وَمَنْ يَّدْعُ مَعَ اللهِ اِلٰهًا اٰخَرَ ۙ لَا بُرْهٰنَ لَهٗ بِهٖ فَاِنَّمَا حِسَابُهٗ عِنْدَ رَبِّهٖ ؕ اِنَّهٗ لَا يُفْلِحُ الْكٰفِرُوْنَ ۝ وَقُلْ رَّبِّ اغْفِرْ وَارْحَمْ وَاَنْتَ خَيْرُ الرّٰحِمِيْنَ ۝

Do you think We have created you in jest and that you would not be brought back to us (for accountability)?
Hence, exalted be Allah, The True King. None is worthy of worship besides He, The Lord of The Throne of Honour.

Al Mu'minun 115,118

Significance: Anyone under the influence of an evil spirit — to cure him, any person should recite the above ayaat thrice and "blow" in a glass of water and sprinkle such water on the patient's face. Alternatively, they should be recited thrice next to his ears. Relief will be noticed instantaneously. Insha Allah

B. Surah Al-Fatihah, Ayatul Kursi and the beginning 5 verses of Surah Jinn.

Significance: For someone under the influence of evil spirits, recite Surah Al-Fatihah, Ayatul Kursi and the beginning 5 verses of Surah Jinn. Then blow on clean water and sprinkle it on the afflicted person's face. If the house is also suspected of any influence, the same water could be sprinkled all over the house.

TO DRIVE OUT JINN FROM A HOUSE

Significance: It is reported from Ibnu Qutaibah R.A. that a certain trader went to Basrah to do some buying and selling of dates. On his arrival in Basrah, he began inquiring for a decent accommodation but couldn't find one. After much seeking he came across a vacant house filled with spider webs. On inquiring from the people the reason for its emptiness he was told that a Jinn is believed to be occupying the house. When he approached the landlord, the latter tried to dissuade him by saying; "Why do you want to jeopardise your life? A powerful Jinn lives there! Whoever stayed there hasn't come out alive!" The trader insisted by saying; "Allah I is my helper! Please, I must have the house!"

However, the landlord had no choice but to concede to his request. From here the story is taken up by the trader. He says; "I occupied the house. Late in the night my eyes suddenly opened and I saw a dark human form approaching me, it's eyes bloodshot — as if bright flames were leaping from them. I immediately began reciting Aayatul Kursi. Every sentence I recited was recited by the Jinn (in an attempt to counter attack)... until I reached

وَلَا يَئُوْدُهُ حِفْظُهُمَا ۚ وَهُوَ الْعَلِيُّ الْعَظِيْمُ

This last sentence he could not utter. I began uttering this sentence repeatedly until I saw the form disappearing. No trace of it seemed to have ever existed. I spent the rest of the night in total comfort. In the morning I scrutinised the place where the Jinn was seen... only to find its remains in the form of a small heap of ashes. Then, from nowhere a voice was heard saying; "You have burnt a poweful Jinn to ashes"! I asked; "What caused him to burn"? The voice replied; The verse:

وَلَا يَئُوْدُهُ حِفْظُهُمَا ۚ وَهُوَ الْعَلِيُّ الْعَظِيْمُ

Their preserving never makes Him weary.
He is The Sublime, The Great.

IMAM AWZA'I R.A. AND THE EVIL JINN

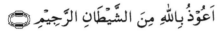

I seek Allah's refuge from the devil accursed.

Significance: Imam Awza'i R.A. is reported to have said that once an evil Jinn suddenly confronted him, frightening him tremendously. He immediately recited the above ayah. The Jinn escaped, crying: "You have sought refuge from The Great! You have sought refuge from The Great!"

TO OVERPOWER ONE'S OPPONENT IN DEBATE

يَاَيُّهَا النَّاسُ قَدْ جَآءَكُمْ بُرْهٰنٌ مِّنْ رَّبِّكُمْ وَاَنْزَلْنَآ اِلَيْكُمْ نُوْرًا مُّبِيْنًا ۞ فَاَمَّا الَّذِيْنَ اٰمَنُوْا بِاللّٰهِ وَاعْتَصَمُوْا بِهٖ فَسَيُدْخِلُهُمْ فِيْ رَحْمَةٍ مِّنْهُ وَفَضْلٍ وَّيَهْدِيْهِمْ اِلَيْهِ صِرَاطًا مُّسْتَقِيْمًا ۞

O mankind! there assuredly has come to you a clear proof from your Lord and We have sent down to

you a light manifest that guides you to the straight path.
Verily those who believe in Allah, and hold fast to His Rope, very soon Allah shall cause them to enter His Mercy and Grace and shall guide them to a straight path towards Himself.

An Nisa 174,175

Significance: *To overcome an enemy in an argument one should recite the above verse.*

TO OVERCOME A FOE IN ANY CONTEST OR BATTLE

Suratul-feel

Significance: *Recitation of Suratul-feel will ensure victory for its reciters when fighting the enemy.*

Ayatul Kursi

Significance: *If Ayatul Kursi is recited before a battle, victory is a certainty, Insha Allah.*

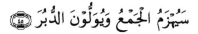

The hosts will be defeated and they will turn their backs and flee.

Al Qamar 45

Significance: Reciting the above ayah and blowing on soil, then throwing such soil in the direction of the enemy will ensure defeat of the enemy.

D. وَمَا رَمَيْتَ اِذْ رَمَيْتَ وَلٰكِنَّ اللّٰهَ رَمٰى ۚ وَلِيُبْلِىَ الْمُؤْمِنِيْنَ مِنْهُ بَلَآءً حَسَنًا ۗ اِنَّ اللّٰهَ سَمِيْعٌ عَلِيْمٌ ۝

اِذَا زُلْزِلَتِ الْاَرْضُ زِلْزَالَهَا ۝ وَاَخْرَجَتِ الْاَرْضُ اَثْقَالَهَا ۝ وَقَالَ الْاِنْسَانُ مَا لَهَا ۝ يَوْمَئِذٍ تُحَدِّثُ اَخْبَارَهَا ۝ بِاَنَّ رَبَّكَ اَوْحٰى لَهَا ۝ يَوْمَئِذٍ يَصْدُرُ النَّاسُ اَشْتَاتًا ەْ

O My Apostle! the dust that you did throw, it was not you who threw it at them when you threw, but Allah threw in order to bestow a favour upon the Believers,

a goodly favour from His Presence.
Verily Allah is the All-Hearing, the All-Knowing.
When the earth is shaken to its utmost shaking -
And the earth throws up her burdens -
And man says (distressed): "What has happened to it?" On that Day it shall narrate all its news For your Lord has (so) commanded it.
On that Day people will return towards their Lord,

Significance: Ibnul Kalbi reports that a very reliable person once told him about Muslims of a certain town besieged by the kuffar. A pious person amongst the Muslims recited the above verses and 'blew' on a handful of soil and had the soil scattered in the camping grounds of the enemy. The result was that the enemy began fighting amongst themselves and dispersed.

BARAKAH IN PRODUCE, LIVESTOCK, ETC.

اَللّٰهُ الَّذِیْ خَلَقَ السَّمٰوٰتِ وَالْاَرْضَ وَاَنْزَلَ مِنَ السَّمَآءِ مَآءً فَاَخْرَجَ بِهٖ مِنَ الثَّمَرٰتِ رِزْقًا لَّكُمْ ۚ وَسَخَّرَ لَكُمُ الْفُلْكَ لِتَجْرِيَ فِي الْبَحْرِ بِاَمْرِهٖ ۚ وَسَخَّرَ لَكُمُ الْاَنْهٰرَ ۝ وَسَخَّرَ لَكُمُ الشَّمْسَ وَالْقَمَرَ دَآئِبَيْنِ ۚ وَسَخَّرَ لَكُمُ الَّيْلَ وَالنَّهَارَ ۝ وَاٰتٰكُمْ مِّنْ كُلِّ مَا سَاَلْتُمُوْهُ ؕ وَاِنْ تَعُدُّوْا نِعْمَتَ اللّٰهِ لَا تُحْصُوْهَا ؕ اِنَّ الْاِنْسٰنَ لَظَلُوْمٌ كَفَّارٌ ۝

*Allah is He Who has created the heavens and the earth and sends down
water (rain) from the sky,*

*and thereby brought forth fruits as provision for you; and He has made
the ships to be of service to you,*

>*that they may sail through the sea by His Command;*
>*and He has made rivers (also) to be of service to you.*

*And He has made the sun and the moon, both constantly
pursuing their courses, to be of service to you;*

*and He has made the night and the day, to be of service to you. And He
gave you of all that you asked for, and if you count the Blessings of
Allah,*

>*never will you be able to count them.*
>*Verily! Man is indeed an extreme wrong-doer, a disbeliever.*

Ibrahim 32,34

Significance: *If recited once in the morning, once in the evening and once when going to bed, Allah I will put barakah in his crops, livestock etc. if recited before undertaking a journey Allah I will protect him and his belongings from all calamities.*

BARAKAH IN BUSINESS, FARMING, HOME, ETC.

A.

بِسْمِ اللهِ الرَّحْمٰنِ الرَّحِيْمِ ۞

الٓمٓرٰ تِلْكَ اٰيٰتُ الْكِتٰبِ ۗ وَالَّذِىْٓ اُنْزِلَ اِلَيْكَ مِنْ رَّبِّكَ الْحَقُّ وَلٰكِنَّ اَكْثَرَ النَّاسِ لَا يُؤْمِنُوْنَ ۞ اَللّٰهُ الَّذِىْ رَفَعَ السَّمٰوٰتِ بِغَيْرِ عَمَدٍ تَرَوْنَهَا ثُمَّ اسْتَوٰى عَلَى الْعَرْشِ وَسَخَّرَ الشَّمْسَ وَالْقَمَرَ ۗ كُلٌّ يَّجْرِىْ لِاَجَلٍ مُّسَمًّى ۗ يُدَبِّرُ الْاَمْرَ يُفَصِّلُ الْاٰيٰتِ لَعَلَّكُمْ بِلِقَآءِ رَبِّكُمْ تُوْقِنُوْنَ ۞

وَهُوَ الَّذِىْ مَدَّ الْاَرْضَ وَجَعَلَ فِيْهَا رَوَاسِىَ وَاَنْهٰرًا ۗ وَمِنْ كُلِّ الثَّمَرٰتِ جَعَلَ فِيْهَا زَوْجَيْنِ اثْنَيْنِ يُغْشِى الَّيْلَ النَّهَارَ ۗ اِنَّ فِىْ ذٰلِكَ لَاٰيٰتٍ لِّقَوْمٍ يَّتَفَكَّرُوْنَ ۞

48

In the name of Allah, Most Beneficent, Most Merciful.
Alif- Lam- Mim- Ra.
These are the Verses of the Divine Book.
And that which has been sent down to you from your Lord is the Truth, but most of the people believe not (because of their wrong-headedness). Allah it is (the Mighty and the Wise) Who has raised the heavens without pillars (as) you see them,
then He settled (Himself) on the Throne of Power, and made the sun and the moon subservient to His command.
Each one running its course to an appointed term.
He plans every affair, and explains clearly His Signs that haply you maybe certain of the Meeting with your Lord.
And He it is Who has spread the earth, and set therein firm mountains and rivers.
And fruits of every kind He has made therein in pairs, two and two. He covers the day with the night.
Verily in all these are Signs of His Might for a people who reflect.

Ar Ra'ad 1,3

Significance: *For progress and barakah in one's business, recite these verses.*

TO DRIVE AWAY PESTS

وَقَالَ الَّذِينَ كَفَرُوا لِرُسُلِهِمْ لَنُخْرِجَنَّكُمْ مِّنْ اَرْضِنَآ اَوْ لَتَعُوْدُنَّ فِيْ مِلَّتِنَا ۖ فَاَوْحٰٓى اِلَيْهِمْ رَبُّهُمْ لَنُهْلِكَنَّ الظّٰلِمِيْنَ ۙ ﴿١٣﴾ وَلَنُسْكِنَنَّكُمُ الْاَرْضَ مِنْۢ بَعْدِهِمْ ۚ ذٰلِكَ لِمَنْ خَافَ مَقَامِيْ وَخَافَ وَعِيْدِ ﴿١٤﴾ وَاسْتَفْتَحُوْا وَخَابَ كُلُّ جَبَّارٍ عَنِيْدٍ ۙ ﴿١٥﴾ مِّنْ وَّرَآئِهٖ جَهَنَّمُ وَيُسْقٰى مِنْ مَّآءٍ صَدِيْدٍ ۙ ﴿١٦﴾ يَّتَجَرَّعُهٗ وَلَا يَكَادُ يُسِيْغُهٗ وَيَاْتِيْهِ الْمَوْتُ مِنْ كُلِّ مَكَانٍ وَّمَا هُوَ بِمَيِّتٍ ۖ وَمِنْ وَّرَآئِهٖ عَذَابٌ غَلِيْظٌ ﴿١٧﴾

> And the infidels said to their Apostles:
> "We will surely drive you out of our country or you will have to come back to our religion."
>
> So their Lord revealed to them: "(Fear not) We will certainly destroy these wrongdoers- "And We shall certainly settle you in their country after (destroying) them.
>
> This (promise of success) is for him who fears the time when he shall before Me and who fears My Warning." And the Apostles begged for success of the Truth (which was granted) and every obstinate rejector of Truth was disappointed- After this (disappointment) is Hell and he will be made to drink blood and water of oozing pus -
>
> Which he will drink little by little with difficulty, and will not be able to swallow it down his throat and death will come to him from every side but (in spite of it) he will not die.
>
> And before him will be another dreadful torment.   Ibrahim 13,17

Significance: If crops are being destroyed by pests such as mice, worms, locust etc. then the above verses should be recited.

B. Surah Al-Tatfif

Significance: To drive out white ants from any grain and legumes such as rice, lentils beans etc. Surah Al-Tatfif (30th Juz) should be recited and "blown" on such foodstuff. They will disappear in a short period — Insha-Allah.

FOR BARAKAH AND PROGRESS IN BUSINESS

A. اِنَّ اللّٰهَ اشْتَرٰى مِنَ الْمُؤْمِنِيْنَ اَنْفُسَهُمْ وَاَمْوَالَهُمْ بِاَنَّ لَهُمُ الْجَنَّةَ ۚ يُقَاتِلُوْنَ فِىْ سَبِيْلِ اللّٰهِ فَيَقْتُلُوْنَ وَيُقْتَلُوْنَ ۖ وَعْدًا عَلَيْهِ حَقًّا فِى التَّوْرٰىةِ وَالْاِنْجِيْلِ وَالْقُرْاٰنِ ۚ وَمَنْ اَوْفٰى بِعَهْدِهٖ مِنَ اللّٰهِ فَاسْتَبْشِرُوْا بِبَيْعِكُمُ الَّذِىْ بَايَعْتُمْ بِهٖ ۚ وَذٰلِكَ هُوَ الْفَوْزُ الْعَظِيْمُ ۝

Certainly Allah has purchased of the Muslims their lives and their wealth that for them in return is the Garden - the fight in the Way of Allah; so they slay and are slain.

Allah has given a solemn promise binding thereon in the Torah, and the Gospel and the Qur'an (all the three Books). And who is more faithful to his promise than Allah?

Rejoice, therefore, (O Believers!) in the bargain that you have struck with Allah.

And that is indeed the supreme achievement.

At Tawbah 111

Significance: Recite the above verse for barakah and protection.

FOR PROGRESS AND PROTECTION IN BUSINESS

Significance: If Ayatul-Kursi is recited and "blown" on one's merchandise the following benefits will be reaped:

a. the merchandise will prove beneficial for its owner;
b. one will make good progress;
c. one will be protected from the mischief and evil promoting of Shaytan;
d. a poor person will become wealthy;
e. sustenance (rizq) will be acquired from strange and unknown sources.

If recited on entering the house and when going to bed:

a. no thieves will enter such a house;
b. the reader will not drown, burn or die due to an accident;
c. he will enjoy good health.

TO KEEP JUSTICE

اِنَّ اللّٰهَ يَأْمُرُ بِالْعَدْلِ وَالْاِحْسَانِ وَإِيْتَآئِ ذِى الْقُرْبٰى وَيَنْهٰى عَنِ الْفَحْشَآءِ وَالْمُنْكَرِ وَالْبَغْيِ يَعِظُكُمْ لَعَلَّكُمْ تَذَكَّرُوْنَ ۞

Allah enjoins adl (justice and worshipping none but Allah alone) and ihsaan (to be patient in performing your duties to Allah,
totally for Allah's sake and in accordance with sunnah) and giving help to kith and kin

(i.e. to give them financial assistance, visiting them, caring for them)

and He forbids you from fahshaa

(sins, evil deeds, illicit sex, disobedience to parents, lies, etc.) and from munkar (all that is prohibited by the shari'ah) and from baghya (oppression of all kinds). He admonishes you so you may take heed.

Significance: *Abdullah bin Umar t narrated that once Umar t asked the people: "Who will tell me which verse in the Holy Qur'an is the greatest? And which verse will spur people to be just and fair? And which verse is most effective in instilling fear into the hearts of people? And which verse is most effective in building the hopes of people?" No one answered. Abdullah bin Mas'ud t finally responded by saying that he heard Rasulullah r saying on the mimbar that the greatest verse of the Holy Qur'an is Ayatul Kursi; and the above verse most effective in urging people to be just.*

FOR LESSENING ONE'S BURDEN

A. اَلْـٰنَ خَفَّفَ اللّٰهُ عَنْكُمْ وَعَلِمَ اَنَّ فِيْكُمْ ضَعْفًا ۚ فَاِنْ يَّكُنْ مِّنْكُمْ مِّائَةٌ صَابِرَةٌ يَّغْلِبُوْا مِائَتَيْنِ ۚ وَاِنْ يَّكُنْ مِّنْكُمْ اَلْفٌ يَّغْلِبُوْٓا اَلْفَيْنِ بِاِذْنِ اللّٰهِ ۚ وَاللّٰهُ مَعَ الصّٰبِرِيْنَ ۞

*Now has Allah lightened Your burden for He knows that there is weakness in you.
So if there be of you, a hundred steadfast, they shall overcome two hundred and if there be of you a thousand
they shall overcome two thousand by the permission of Allah. And Allah is with the steadfast.*

Al Anfal 66

Significance: *A person doing hard, menial work or carrying burdens on his back or doing any work that demands physical or mental exertion — if he is desirous of lessening his burden and simplifying his task — he should recite the above verse once after every Salaah for one week. He should start on any Friday after Asr Salaah and continue till the following Friday after Jumu'ah Salaah. Insha Allah, all his tasks will become easy.*

WHEN ENTERING A TOWN

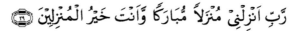

O My Lord cause me to land at a blessed place for You are the best of all who bring to land.

Al Mu'minun 29

Significance: Recite the above verse on entering any town, city or village. One's stay in such a place will be a pleasant one. Insha Allah

WHEN BOARDING ANY MEANS OF CONVEYANCE/ TRANSPORT

سُبْحٰنَ الَّذِىْ سَخَّرَ لَنَا هٰذَا وَمَا كُنَّا لَهٗ مُقْرِنِيْنَ ۝

Glorified be He who has subdued these for us and we were not capable of subduing them.

Az Zukhruf 13

Significance: If the above verse is recited before boarding a vehicle, train, aircraft, ship etc. one will be protected from all forms of calamities. Insha Allah.

PROTECTION OF A VESSEL

A.

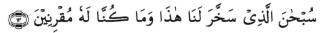

بِسْمِ اللهِ مَجْرٖىهَا وَمُرْسٰىهَاۤ ؕ اِنَّ رَبِّىْ لَغَفُوْرٌ رَّحِيْمٌ ۝

*In the Name of Allah be its course and its mooring.
Lo! My Lord is Most Forgiving, Ever Merciful.*

Hud 41

Significance: The above ayah should be recited before embarking a ship or boat. The ship and all its occupants will be safeguarded against all calamities. Insha Allah.

B. وَقَالَ ارْكَبُوْا فِيْهَا بِسْمِ اللّٰهِ مَجْرٖىهَا وَمُرْسٰىهَاۗ اِنَّ رَبِّىْ لَغَفُوْرٌ رَّحِيْمٌ ۝

And he said: Embark therein. With the Name of Allah, be its course and it's mooring. Lo! my Lord is Most Forgiving, Ever Merciful.

Hud 41

Significance: *This verse should also be recited before embarking the vessel.*

C. Surah Luqman

Significance: *Surah Luqman (Juz 21). If recited before embarking a vessel, a person will be safeguarded against drowning. Insha Allah.*

WHEN THE SEAS ARE ROUGH

A. اَلَمْ تَرَ اَنَّ الْفُلْكَ تَجْرِىْ فِى الْبَحْرِ بِنِعْمَتِ اللهِ لِيُرِيَكُمْ مِّنْ اٰيٰتِهٖ ۚ اِنَّ فِىْ ذٰلِكَ لَاٰيٰتٍ لِّكُلِّ صَبَّارٍ شَكُوْرٍ ﴿۳۱﴾

Have you not seen how the ships glide on the sea by Allah's grace that He may show you of His wonders! Lo! indeed, therein are signs for every steadfast, grateful (soul). Luqman 31

Significance: *When the seas become rough and there is fear of disaster, the above ayah should be recited. Insha Allah the seas will become calm.*

FOR RETURNING HOME SAFE AND SOUND

A. اَلْعَلِىُّ

The High

Significance: *If a wayfarer (musafir) keeps a written copy of above name of Allah I he will return to his people in a short period of time. Insha Allah — Moreover, if he is needy, Allah will grant him abundant wealth.*

B. اَلْاَوَّلُ

The First

Significance: *If a musafir reads above name of Allah 1000 times every Friday, he will return to his people safely, Insha Allah.*

FEVER

A. اِنَّ الَّذِيْنَ اتَّقَوْا اِذَا مَسَّهُمْ طٰٓئِفٌ مِّنَ الشَّيْطٰنِ تَذَكَّرُوْا فَاِذَا هُمْ مُّبْصِرُوْنَ ۝

Surely those who ward off evil when a glamour from the devil troubles them, they remember Allah and behold; they are people of insight.

Al A'raf 201

Significance: *The above could be recited and 'blown' on a person who has a fever due to heat. Insha Allah he will soon be cured through the barakah of the words of Allah.*

B. قُلْنَا يٰنَارُ كُوْنِيْ بَرْدًا وَّسَلٰمًا عَلٰٓى اِبْرٰهِيْمَ ۝

We said: "O Fire! Become cool and peaceful for Ibrahim!" Al Ambiya 69

Significance: *The above should be recited near a sick person. Insha Allah, the fever will subside.*

FOR ANY SICKNESS

A.

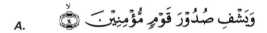

And He will cure the breast of people who believe.

At Tauba 14

وَشِفَآءٌ لِّمَا فِى الصُّدُوْرِ

And (the Qur'an) is a cure for ailments which prevail in the hearts.

Yunus 57

يَخْرُجُ مِنْ بُطُوْنِهَا شَرَابٌ مُّخْتَلِفٌ اَلْوَانُهٗ فِيْهِ شِفَآءٌ لِّلنَّاسِ

There comes forth from their (the bees) bellies a drink (honey) diverse of colours, wherein is healing for mankind.

An Nahl 69

وَنُنَزِّلُ مِنَ الْقُرْاٰنِ مَا هُوَ شِفَآءٌ وَّرَحْمَةٌ لِّلْمُؤْمِنِيْنَ

And we reveal of the Qur'an that which is a source of healing and a source of mercy for the Believers.

Bani Israil 82

وَاِذَا مَرِضْتُ فَهُوَ يَشْفِيْنِ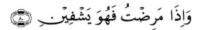

And when I am sick, then He heals me.

Ash Shu'araa 80

قُلْ هُوَ لِلَّذِيْنَ اٰمَنُوْا هُدًى وَّشِفَآءٌ

Say unto them (O Muhammad!):

For those who believe, it (the Qur'an) is a guidance and a healing.
Fussilat 44

Significance: The above verses should be recited. Insha Allah he will be cured even if the sickness is of a serious nature.

B. وَنُنَزِّلُ مِنَ الْقُرْاٰنِ مَا هُوَ شِفَآءٌ وَّرَحْمَةٌ لِّلْمُؤْمِنِيْنَ

And we reveal of the Qur'an that which is a source of healing and a source of mercy for the Believers.

Bani Israil 82

Significance: *The above ayah should be read and blown on the patient.*

TO REMOVE PAIN

Significance: *To relieve a patient of any pain, Surah Yasin should be read.*

TO CURE INSOMNIA

Significance: *To enable a patient to get a good sleep, Surah Mujadalah (Juz 28) should be recited next to the patient.*

MORE PRESCRIPTIONS FOR ALL TYPES OF AILMENTS

A. اَلسَّلَامُ

The Giver of Peace

Significance: *Stand by the head side of a patient and lifting the hands as in Du'a, say the above Name of Allah I 39 times in such a manner that the patient hears it. Insha Allah, he will soon be cured.*

B. اَلْعَظِيْمُ

The Great

Significance: *Saying the above name of Allah I excessively will remove any sickness.*

C. اَلْحَىُّ

The Ever-Living

Significance: *The above Beautiful Name of Allah I should either be recited excessively or it should be written on paper with saffron and after washing it, the water should be consumed.*

D. اَلْغَنِيُّ

The Independent

Significance: *The above Name of Allah I to be recited excessively at the time of any calamity or sickness. Recovery should be expected in a short time. Insha Allah.*

FOR MELANCHOLY AND DEPRESSION

A. وَلِيَرْبِطَ عَلٰى قُلُوْبِكُمْ وَيُثَبِّتَ بِهِ الْاَقْدَامَ ۝

To make strong you hearts and to keep your feet firm thereby.

Al Anfal 17

B. اَلَّذِيْنَ اٰمَنُوْا وَتَطْمَئِنُّ قُلُوْبُهُمْ بِذِكْرِ اللّٰهِ ۗ اَلَا بِذِكْرِ اللّٰهِ تَطْمَئِنُّ الْقُلُوْبُ ۝

Who have believed and whose hearts are at ease in the remembrance of Allah.
Verily in the remembrance of Allah do hearts find rest. Ar Rad 28

Significance: *The above ayaat is very effective for removing melancholy and depression.*

PALPITATION OF THE HEART

اَفَغَيْرَ دِيْنِ اللّٰهِ يَبْغُوْنَ وَلَهٗٓ اَسْلَمَ مَنْ فِى السَّمٰوٰتِ وَالْاَرْضِ طَوْعًا وَّكَرْهًا وَّاِلَيْهِ يُرْجَعُوْنَ ۝ قُلْ اٰمَنَّا بِاللّٰهِ وَمَآ اُنْزِلَ عَلَيْنَا وَمَآ اُنْزِلَ عَلٰٓى اِبْرٰهِيْمَ وَاِسْمٰعِيْلَ وَاِسْحٰقَ وَيَعْقُوْبَ وَالْاَسْبَاطِ وَمَآ اُوْتِىَ مُوْسٰى وَعِيْسٰى وَالنَّبِيُّوْنَ مِنْ رَّبِّهِمْ لَا نُفَرِّقُ بَيْنَ اَحَدٍ مِّنْهُمْ وَنَحْنُ لَهٗ مُسْلِمُوْنَ ۝ وَمَنْ يَّبْتَغِ غَيْرَ الْاِسْلَامِ دِيْنًا فَلَنْ يُّقْبَلَ مِنْهُ وَهُوَ فِى الْاٰخِرَةِ مِنَ الْخٰسِرِيْنَ ۝

> Do they seek (a religion) other than the Religion of Allah?
> Yet to Him has submitted whosoever is in the heavens and in the earth, willingly or unwillingly,
> and to Him shall they (all) be brought back in the end.
> Say (O Muslims!): "We believe in Allah and what has been sent down to us, and that which was sent down to Abraham and
> Ishamael and Isaaq and Jacob and their offspring and what was given to Moses and Jesus and the other Prophets from their Lord.
> We make no distinction between any of them, in the matter of faith and to Allah have we surrendered ourselves."
> And whosoever seeks a religion other than Islam, it shall certainly not be accepted of him; and in the Hereafter he shall be of the losers.

Al Imran 83,85

Significance: The above verses are said to be most effective for the softening of the heart.

AILMENT OF THE HEART

Surah Al-Inshirah

Significance: Recite Surah Al-Inshirah (30th Juz) and blow on the patient.

STRENGTHENING THE HEART

اَلْمَاجِدُ

The Excellent

Significance: If the above beautiful name of Allah I is recited a number of times and blown on a morsel before eating it, the heart will be strengthened — Insha Allah.

TO ACQUIRE FREEDOM FROM MATERIALISM

A. اَلْوَاحِدُالْأَحَدُ

The One And Only

Significance: To acquire independence in the heart recite the above name of Allah I 1000 times. The importance of material objects will depart from the reader's heart.

DISEASE OF THE SPLEEN

اِنَّ اللّٰهَ يُمْسِكُ السَّمٰوٰتِ وَالْاَرْضَ اَنْ تَزُوْلَا ۚ وَلَئِنْ زَالَتَآ اِنْ اَمْسَكَهُمَا مِنْ اَحَدٍ مِّنْۢ بَعْدِهٖ ؕ اِنَّهٗ كَانَ حَلِيْمًا غَفُوْرًا ۝

*Lo! Allah grasps the heaven and the earth that they deviate not.
And if they were to deviate there is not one that could grasp it after that.*

Lo! He is For-Ever Clement, Forgiving.

Fatir 41

Significance: Read the above ayah on paper and rub the portion where the spleen is situated. Insha Allah the disease will be removed.

FOR A SPECIFIC PAIN

A.

وَبِالْحَقِّ اَنْزَلْنٰهُ وَبِالْحَقِّ نَزَلَ ۔ وَمَآ اَرْسَلْنٰكَ اِلَّا مُبَشِّرًا وَّنَذِيْرًا ۞

With truth have we revealed it and with truth it has descended. And we have not sent you but as a bearer of good tidings and as a warner.

Bani Israil 105

Significance: Place the hand on the portion where the pain is felt and recite the above ayah once and blow thrice on the affected area. Insha Allah the pain will disappear.

B.

بِسْمِ اللّٰهِ الرَّحْمٰنِ الرَّحِيْمِ ۞

اَلْحَمْدُ لِلّٰهِ الَّذِيْ خَلَقَ السَّمٰوٰتِ وَالْاَرْضَ وَجَعَلَ الظُّلُمٰتِ وَالنُّوْرَ ثُمَّ الَّذِيْنَ كَفَرُوْا بِرَبِّهِمْ يَعْدِلُوْنَ ۞

In the name of Allah, Most Beneficent, Most Merciful. Praise be to Allah, who has created the heavens and the earth and has appointed darkness and light. Yet those who disbelieve ascribe rivals unto their Lord.   Al An'am 1

Significance: A person who recites the above ayah 7 times in the morning and 7 times in the evening, then blows on his hands and passes them all over his body, will be safeguarded against all pains and physical calamities.

HEADACHES

A.

لَّا يُصَدَّعُوْنَ عَنْهَا وَلَا يُنْزِفُوْنَ ۞

Where from they get no aching of the head nor any madness.

Al Waqiah 19

Significance: Recite the above verse thrice and blow on the patient. The headache will disappear — Insha Allah.

B.

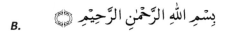

In the name of Allah, Most Beneficent, Most Merciful

Significance: It is reported that the king of Rome once complained to Umar t about his persistent headache. The Khalifah had a hat (topi) sewn for him. Whenever the king wore it, his headache disappeared. And whenever he took it off, it returned. He became wholly astonished. Curiosity made him open the seams of the headgear, to find the words "Bismillah" written beneath the seams.

MIGRAINE

A. Surah Takathur

Significance: Recite Surah Takathur (30th Juz) after Asr Salaah and blow on the head of the patient. This is a very effective remedy for migraine.

B. قُلْ مَنْ رَّبُّ السَّمٰوٰتِ وَالْاَرْضِ ۭ قُلِ اللّٰهُ ۭ قُلْ اَفَاتَّخَذْتُمْ مِّنْ دُوْنِهٖۤ اَوْلِيَآءَ لَا يَمْلِكُوْنَ لِاَنْفُسِهِمْ نَفْعًا وَّلَا ضَرًّا ۭ

Say: Who is the Master of the heavens and earth?
Say: Allah! Say: Yet you take other than Him as friends who possess no power over themselves in giving benefit and difficulty?

Ar Ra'ad 16

Significance: *Recite the above ayah and blow on the patient. Insha Allah, the migraine will disappear.*

INFLAMMATION OF THE EYES

A. اَللّٰهُ نُوْرُ السَّمٰوٰتِ وَالْاَرْضِ ؕ مَثَلُ نُوْرِهٖ كَمِشْكٰوةٍ فِيْهَا مِصْبَاحٌ ؕ اَلْمِصْبَاحُ فِيْ زُجَاجَةٍ ؕ اَلزُّجَاجَةُ كَاَنَّهَا كَوْكَبٌ دُرِّيٌّ يُّوْقَدُ مِنْ شَجَرَةٍ مُّبٰرَكَةٍ زَيْتُوْنَةٍ لَّا شَرْقِيَّةٍ وَّلَا غَرْبِيَّةٍ ۙ يَّكَادُ زَيْتُهَا يُضِيْٓءُ وَلَوْ لَمْ تَمْسَسْهُ نَارٌ ؕ نُوْرٌ عَلٰى نُوْرٍ ؕ يَهْدِى اللّٰهُ لِنُوْرِهٖ مَنْ يَّشَآءُ ؕ وَيَضْرِبُ اللّٰهُ الْاَمْثَالَ لِلنَّاسِ ؕ وَاللّٰهُ بِكُلِّ شَيْءٍ عَلِيْمٌ ۙ﴿٣٥﴾ فِيْ بُيُوْتٍ اَذِنَ اللّٰهُ اَنْ تُرْفَعَ وَيُذْكَرَ فِيْهَا اسْمُهٗ ۙ يُسَبِّحُ لَهٗ فِيْهَا بِالْغُدُوِّ وَالْاٰصَالِ ۙ﴿٣٦﴾ رِجَالٌ ۙ لَّا تُلْهِيْهِمْ تِجَارَةٌ وَّلَا بَيْعٌ عَنْ ذِكْرِ اللّٰهِ وَاِقَامِ الصَّلٰوةِ وَاِيْتَآءِ الزَّكٰوةِ ۪ۙ يَخَافُوْنَ يَوْمًا تَتَقَلَّبُ فِيْهِ الْقُلُوْبُ وَالْاَبْصَارُ ۙ﴿٣٧﴾ لِيَجْزِيَهُمُ اللّٰهُ اَحْسَنَ مَا عَمِلُوْا وَيَزِيْدَهُمْ مِّنْ فَضْلِهٖ ؕ وَاللّٰهُ يَرْزُقُ مَنْ يَّشَآءُ بِغَيْرِ حِسَابٍ ﴿٣٨﴾

Allah is the Light of the heavens and the earth.

The likeness of His light is as a niche wherein is a lamp, that lamp is in (a chandelier of) glass, the chandelier is as a star glittering like a pearl lit from a blessed olive tree,

neither eastern nor western, whose oil is almost luminous even though no fire touches it.

(This) is all light upon light!
Allah guides unto His light whom
He will, And Allah sets forth all manner of parables for (the guidance of) mankind.

And verily Allah is Best Knower of all things.

In the houses (of worship) which Allah has ordered to be exalted, and His name to be remembered therein - extol His Glory therein in the mornings and the evenings -

By men whom neither trade nor business diverts from the Remembrance of Allah, and the establishing of prayer and the paying of the poor-rate (Zakaat).

They keep fearing the Day when hearts will be unnerved and eyes convulsed (with terror)-

That Allah may recompense them for their best deeds, and may grant them still more out of His Grace. And Allah provides for those whom He will, without measure.

An Nur 35,39

Significance: *A person who continually suffers from inflammation of the eyes (conjunctivitis) should recite the above verses thrice daily after Fajr salaah and blow on the back of both thumbs and rub onto both eyes. He will be cured in due course, Insha Allah.*

B. Surah Al-Mulk

Significance: Surah Al-Mulk should be recited thrice each day for 3 consecutive days. After reciting it 3 times blow on the patient's eyes. The suffering will be alleviated — Insha Allah.

STRENGTHENING THE EYESIGHT

A.
فَكَشَفْنَا عَنْكَ غِطَآءَكَ فَبَصَرُكَ الْيَوْمَ حَدِيدٌ ۝

Now We have removed from you your veil and this day your sight is iron.

Qaf 22

Significance: Recite this verse thrice after every salaah, blow on the fingers and rub them on the eyes. By doing this the eyesight will never weaken. In fact, any weakness will also disappear.

B.

بِسْمِ اللهِ الرَّحْمٰنِ الرَّحِيْمِ ۝

اِنَّآ اَنْزَلْنٰهُ فِیْ لَیْلَةِ الْقَدْرِ ۝ وَمَآ اَدْرٰىكَ مَا لَیْلَةُ الْقَدْرِ ۝ لَیْلَةُ الْقَدْرِ ۬ خَیْرٌ مِّنْ اَلْفِ شَہْرٍ ۝ تَنَزَّلُ الْمَلٰٓئِكَةُ وَالرُّوْحُ فِیْہَا بِاِذْنِ رَبِّہِمْ ۚ مِّنْ كُلِّ اَمْرٍ ۝ سَلٰمٌ ۟ ھِیَ حَتّٰی مَطْلَعِ الْفَجْرِ ۝

No doubt, We sent down this blessed Qur'an in Night of Power.
And what will explain to you know what the Night of Power if? The Night of
Power is better than a thousand months.
The angels and the (Holy) Spirit (Gabriel) descend in it by the Command of their
Lord for every affair (of good).
It is all (peace and) security till the rise of the dawn. Al Qadr 1,5

Significance: Anyone who gazes towards the sky while in the state of Wudhu and reads the above Surah, his eyesight will never weaken — Insha Allah.

PAIN IN THE KIDNEY

Significance: Recite Surah Quraish (30th Juz) and blow on any food before consuming it. The pain will disappear — Insha Allah.

EPILEPSY

A. بِسْمِ اللهِ الرَّحْمٰنِ الرَّحِيْمِ آلمَصٓ طٰسٓمٓ كٓهٰيٰعٓصٓ

يٰسٓ وَالْقُرْاٰنِ الْحَكِيْمِ حٰمٓ عٓسٓقٓ نٓ وَالْقَلَمِ وَمَا يَسْطُرُوْنَ

Significance: It is reported of a certain sage that his domestic servant had continuous bouts of epileptic fits. On one such occasion he recited the above words of the Holy Qur'an in her ears. She immediately came to and never had the attack all her life.

B. Surah Ash-Shams

Significance: Reciting Surah Ash-Shams (30th Juz) in the patient's ear is believed to be very beneficial for epilepsy.

PARALYSIS OF THE BODY

A. هُوَ اللّٰهُ الَّذِىْ لَآ اِلٰهَ اِلَّا هُوَ ۚ عٰلِمُ الْغَيْبِ وَالشَّهَادَةِ ۚ هُوَالرَّحْمٰنُ الرَّحِيْمُ ۝ هُوَ اللّٰهُ الَّذِىْ لَآ اِلٰهَ اِلَّا هُوَ ۚ اَلْمَلِكُ الْقُدُّوْسُ السَّلٰمُ الْمُؤْمِنُ الْمُهَيْمِنُ الْعَزِيْزُ الْجَبَّارُ الْمُتَكَبِّرُ ۭ سُبْحٰنَ اللّٰهِ عَمَّا يُشْرِكُوْنَ ۝ هُوَ اللّٰهُ الْخَالِقُ الْبَارِئُ الْمُصَوِّرُ لَهُ الْاَسْمَآءُ الْحُسْنٰى ۭ يُسَبِّحُ لَهٗ مَا فِى السَّمٰوٰتِ وَالْاَرْضِ ۚ وَهُوَ الْعَزِيْزُ الْحَكِيْمُ ۝

وَنُنَزِّلُ مِنَ الْقُرْاٰنِ مَا هُوَ شِفَآءٌ وَّرَحْمَةٌ لِّلْمُؤْمِنِيْنَ وَلَا يَزِيْدُ الظّٰلِمِيْنَ اِلَّا خَسَارًا ۝

He is Allah, besides Whom there is none to be worshipped; Knower of everything hidden and open.

He it is the Most-Kind, the Ever-Merciful.

He is Allah-besides Whom there is none to be worshipped; the Sovereign of all, the Most Holy, the Bestower of Peace,

the Giver of Security, the Guardian over all, the Esteemed One, the Mender of broken hearts, the Exalted in Might.

Glory be to Allah from what they associate with Him.

He is Allah, the Creator of all, the Maker of all,

the Fashioner of all, His are all most beautiful names,

Whatever is in the heavens and the earth glorifies Him; and He it is - the All-Powerful, the All-Wise.

And We send down in the Qur'an that which is a (means of) healing and a mercy to the Believers from end to end,

and the Qur'an only increases the wrongdoers in loss.

Significance: Ibnu Qutaibah R.A. reports that he once inquired from a person who was completely cured from paralysis, the secret to his cure. He replied that he had blown on Zam water and drank it. He was completely cured of his paralysis

LEPROSY

A.

وَاَيُّوْبَ اِذْ نَادٰى رَبَّهٗٓ اَنِّيْ مَسَّنِيَ الضُّرُّ وَاَنْتَ اَرْحَمُ الرّٰحِمِيْنَ ۖ

> And remember Ayyoob when he cried to His Lord:
> "Truly distress has seized me, but You are the Most Merciful of those who are Merciful.

Al Ambiya 83

Significance: Ibnu Qutaibah t reports that a certain leper whose flesh was about to disintegrate, consulted a sage for a cure. The latter recited the relevant verse and blew on him. This caused new skin to appear on his body and he was completely cured. The verse recited by the sage is the above ayah.

B. اَلْمَجِيْدُ

Most Venerable

Significance: *If a leper fasts on the 13th, 14th and 15th of any lunar month and recites the above attribute of Allah I excessively each day at the time of breaking his fast, he will be cured of the disease — Insha Allah.*

C. بِسْمِ اللهِ الرَّحْمٰنِ الرَّحِيْمِ ۞

اَنِّىْ قَدْ جِئْتُكُمْ بِاٰيَةٍ مِّنْ رَّبِّكُمْ ۙ اَنِّىْٓ اَخْلُقُ لَكُمْ مِّنَ الطِّيْنِ كَهَيْئَةِ الطَّيْرِ فَاَنْفُخُ فِيْهِ فَيَكُوْنُ طَيْرًۢا بِاِذْنِ اللهِ ۚ وَاُبْرِئُ الْاَكْمَهَ وَالْاَبْرَصَ وَاُحْيِ الْمَوْتٰى بِاِذْنِ اللهِ ۚ وَاُنَبِّئُكُمْ بِمَا تَاْكُلُوْنَ وَمَا تَدَّخِرُوْنَ ۙ فِىْ بُيُوْتِكُمْ ؕ اِنَّ فِىْ ذٰلِكَ لَاٰيَةً لَّكُمْ اِنْ كُنْتُمْ مُّؤْمِنِيْنَ ۞

In the name of Allah, Most Beneficent, Most Merciful
'Surely I have come to you with a Sign (miracle) from your Lord:
surely I make for you out of clay the form of a bird, then I breathe into
this lifeless form and

it becomes a living bird by the will of Allah;
and I heal the born blind and cure the incurable leper, and bring the
dead to life by the will of Allah; and I declare to you what you eat
and

what you keep stored in your houses -
surely there is a great Sign for you of my truth
in these miracles, if you are true believers.

Al Imr`an 49

Significance: It is reported from Kalbi that a certain person who was afflicted with leprosy related to him that the disease had taken its toll on him to such an extent that he found it embarrassing to sit near anyone owing to the offensive smell his body gave off. However, one day he met a pious person and complained to him about his illness. The sage recited a verse from the Qur'an over water and made him drink it. In a few days he was cured. The verse recited by the sage is the above ayah.

ITCHING OF THE BODY

فَكَسَوْنَا الْعِظٰمَ لَحْمًا ۚ ثُمَّ اَنْشَاْنٰهُ خَلْقًا اٰخَرَ ط

فَتَبَارَكَ اللّٰهُ اَحْسَنُ الْخٰلِقِيْنَ ﴿۞﴾

And We clothed the bones with flesh; then We made it into another creature.

Thus exalted is Allah, The Best of Creators.

Al Mu'minun 14

Significance: *It is reported that a certain person's body itched a great deal owing to some type of rash he suffered from. For a long time he tried all remedies, but to no avail. Finally, one day he decided to join a caravan heading for Makkah. By the time the caravan reached the tomb of Ali t this person became so tired that he decided to remain at the tomb. The caravan left without him. That night he saw and heard Ali t in his dream recite the above verses.*

When he awoke in the morning there was not the slightest trace of the sickness.

BONE FRACTURE

فَاِنْ تَوَلَّوْا فَقُلْ حَسْبِيَ اللّٰهُ لَآ اِلٰهَ اِلَّا هُوَ عَلَيْهِ تَوَكَّلْتُ وَهُوَ رَبُّ الْعَرْشِ الْعَظِيْمِ ۝

*But if they turn away, say: 'Allah suffices me:
There is none worthy of worship but He: upon Him is my trust —
He is Lord of the Great Throne.'*

At Tawbah 129

Significance: *Laith bin Sa'ad R.A. reports that a certain person sustained an injury as a result of which his thigh-bone broke. A man appeared in his dream. He placed his hand on the affected area and recited the above verse. His thigh healed in a short period of time.*

The above verse is also said to be very effective in affording its reader safety against falling from a high place, drowning and being struck by iron. Abud-Darda t is reported as saying that a person who recites it 100 times daily, all his worldly needs and needs pertaining to the hereafter will be fulfilled.

FORGETFULNESS

The Compassionate

Significance: Read the above Beautiful Name of Allah I 100 times after every salaah. Forgetfulness, negligence and stupor will be warded off — Insha Allah.

TO REMOVE HARDHEARTEDNESS

The Most Merciful

Significance: Recite the above attribute of Allah I 100 times every day. Hardheartedness will be replaced with affection, tenderness, kindness and compassion — Insha Allah.

BARAKAH IN FOOD

Significance: A'ishah y reports that a person came to Rasulullah r and complained that there was no barakah blessings in his home. Rasulullah r asked: "Why are you negligent of Ayatul Kursi? Whoever reads it upon any food, Allah I will impart barakah to such food."

THE PRICE OF JANNAH

Significance: Abu Umamah Sa'd ibn Ajalaan t says that Rasulullah r said that anyone who recites Ayatul Kursi after Fardh salaah, the only thing that prevents him from going to Jannah is death.

NIGHTMARES

لَهُمُ الْبُشْرٰى فِى الْحَيٰوةِ الدُّنْيَا وَفِى الْاٰخِرَةِ ۚ لَا تَبْدِيْلَ لِكَلِمٰتِ اللّٰهِ ۚ ذٰلِكَ هُوَ الْفَوْزُ الْعَظِيْمُ ۝

For them are glad tidings in the life of this world and the hereafter.
There is no change in the word of Allah.
This is, without doubt, supreme felicity.

Yunus 64

Significance: The above could be recited before sleeping by one who has continuous nightmares.

INSOMNIA

$$\text{اِنَّ اللهَ وَمَلٰٓئِكَتَهٗ يُصَلُّوْنَ عَلَى النَّبِيِّ ۚ يٰٓاَيُّهَا الَّذِيْنَ اٰمَنُوْا صَلُّوْا عَلَيْهِ وَسَلِّمُوْا تَسْلِيْمًا ۝}$$

Surely, Allah and His angels send salawaat (blessings) on the Nabi. O you who believe,
(you too) send salawaat and salutations on him.

Al Ahzab 56

Significance: To beat insomnia and have a good night's sleep read the above verse excessively.

THE 99 BEAUTIFUL NAMES OF ALLAH I

Significance: Memorising and reading the 99 Beautiful Names of Allah I is an act of great merit. Glad-tidings of admittance into Jannah is given. Any du'a made after its recitation is assuredly accepted. Reciting it after Fajr salaah entails the assured acceptance of du'a and the attraction of Allah's mercy. The method of reciting is to say Jalla Jallaluhu after each attribute of Allah I.

FOR PROTECTION AGAINST THIEVES

اٰمَنَ الرَّسُوۡلُ بِمَاۤ اُنۡزِلَ اِلَيۡهِ مِنۡ رَّبِّهٖ وَالۡمُؤۡمِنُوۡنَ ؕ كُلٌّ اٰمَنَ بِاللّٰهِ وَمَلٰٓئِكَتِهٖ وَكُتُبِهٖ وَرُسُلِهٖ ۫ لَا نُفَرِّقُ بَيۡنَ اَحَدٍ مِّنۡ رُّسُلِهٖ ۫ وَقَالُوۡا سَمِعۡنَا وَاَطَعۡنَا ۗ غُفۡرَانَكَ رَبَّنَا وَاِلَيۡكَ الۡمَصِيۡرُ ﴿۲۸۵﴾ لَا يُكَلِّفُ اللّٰهُ نَفۡسًا اِلَّا وُسۡعَهَا ؕ لَهَا مَا كَسَبَتۡ وَعَلَيۡهَا مَا اكۡتَسَبَتۡ ؕ رَبَّنَا لَا تُؤَاخِذۡنَاۤ اِنۡ نَّسِيۡنَاۤ اَوۡ اَخۡطَاۡنَا ۚ رَبَّنَا وَلَا تَحۡمِلۡ عَلَيۡنَاۤ اِصۡرًا كَمَا حَمَلۡتَهٗ عَلَى الَّذِيۡنَ مِنۡ قَبۡلِنَا ۚ رَبَّنَا وَلَا تُحَمِّلۡنَا مَا لَا طَاقَةَ لَنَا بِهٖ ۚ وَاعۡفُ عَنَّا ۙ وَاغۡفِرۡ لَنَا ۙ وَارۡحَمۡنَا ۚ اَنۡتَ مَوۡلٰىنَا فَانۡصُرۡنَا عَلَى الۡقَوۡمِ الۡكٰفِرِيۡنَ ﴿۲۸۶﴾

The (Holy) Apostle believes in that (Book) which has been sent down to him from his Lord; and so do the believers.

Each one believes in all sincerity in Allah and His Angels and His Books and His Apostles; (and they proclaim):

"We discriminate not against any of His Apostles." And they say: "We hear, and we obey.

We seek Your Forgiveness, O our Lord, and it is You to Whom we all are to return in the end." Allah does not burden any soul with more than it can bear.

For it hall be the reward of what (good) it has earned, and against it shall be (the punishment of) what (evil) it has committed:

"Our Lord! call us not to account if we forget or err. Our Lord! lay not on us such a (heavy) burden as

You did lay on those who have passed away before us.

Our Lord! lay not on us that burden which we have not the strength to bear.

And pardon us; absolve us; and have mercy on us;

You alone are our Friend and Helper; help us to triumph over the unbelieving folk."

Al Baqarah 285, 286

Significance: *Anyone who recites the above verses before going to bed, his wealth, property and life will be safeguarded against all calamities.*

B. AYATUL-KURSI

Significance: *A person who recites Ayatul-Kursi after every salaah, and in the morning and evening, and on entering the house, and when going to bed, he will becomes self-sufficient; Allah will grant him sustenance from unimaginable sources; belongings and property will be protected from burglaries; his sustenance (rizq) will increase; and he will never be afflicted with poverty. And wherever it is recited, burglars would not dare to visit that place.*

C.

فَاِذَا اسْتَوَيْتَ اَنْتَ وَمَنْ مَّعَكَ عَلَى الْفُلْكِ فَقُلِ الْحَمْدُ لِلّٰهِ الَّذِىْ نَجّٰنَا مِنَ الْقَوْمِ الظّٰلِمِيْنَ ۞ وَقُلْ رَّبِّ اَنْزِلْنِىْ مُنْزَلاً مُّبَارَكًا وَّاَنْتَ خَيْرُ الْمُنْزِلِيْنَ ۞

And when you have embarked on the ark — you and those with you
— say:
"Praise be to Allah who has saved us from the people who do
wrong".
And say: "O my Lord, enable me to disembark with (Your) blessings for you
are the best to enable us to disembark".

Al Mu'minun 28,29

Significance: Recitation of the above affords the reciter and his family protection against thieves, enemies and Jinn.

SAFEGUARDING OF MONEY AND VALUABLES

Significance: For safekeeping of money, recite Surah Al-Asr (30th Juz) when banking it or putting it in a safe place or hiding it anywhere. The same applies to valuables.

TO FIND A LOST OBJECT

A.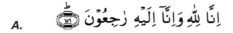

We belong to Allah and to Him shall we return.

Al Baqarah 156

Significance: *Recite the above ayah and search for the lost object. Insha Allah it will be found. Otherwise, something better and greater in value will be received.*

B. Surah Adh-Dhuha

Significance: *Recite Surah Adh-Dhuha (30th Juz) seven times. The lost item will be found — Insha Allah.*

C.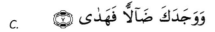

And He found you distracted in His love, so He led you on the way to guidance.

Ad Duha 7

Significance: *Recite Surah Adh-Duha (30th Juz) once. But repeat the above verse thrice. The lost item will be found — Insha Allah.*

FOR THE RETURN OF SOMEONE WHO HAS ABSCONDED

Suratud-Duhaa

Significance: *Recite Suratud-Duhaa seven times. Insha Allah, the runaway will return.*

ENSURING THE SAFETY OF ONE'S FAMILY AND PROPERTY DURING ONE'S ABSENCE

The Guardian

Significance: *Before undertaking a journey, recite the above attribute of Allah I seven times:*

Doing this, there will be no need to worry about their safety until one returns.

PROTECTION AGAINST ALL TYPES OF ANIMALS, INSECTS AND REPTILES

وَكَلْبُهُمْ بٰسِطٌ ذِرَاعَيْهِ بِالْوَصِيْدِ ۚ

And their dog stretching forth his two fore-legs on the threshold.

Al Khaf 18

Significance: When a dog poses a threat — *The following verse should be recited when a dog growls or is about to attack. The same applies to any other wild animal such as a lion, cheetah etc. The above verse.*

PROTECTION AGAINST SNAKES AND SCORPIONS

اِنَّ رَبَّكُمُ اللّٰهُ الَّذِىْ خَلَقَ السَّمٰوٰتِ وَالْاَرْضَ فِىْ سِتَّةِ اَيَّامٍ ثُمَّ اسْتَوٰى عَلَى الْعَرْشِ يُغْشِى الَّيْلَ النَّهَارَ يَطْلُبُهٗ حَثِيْثًا ۙ وَّالشَّمْسَ وَالْقَمَرَ وَالنُّجُوْمَ مُسَخَّرٰتٍۢ بِاَمْرِهٖ ؕ اَلَا لَهُ الْخَلْقُ وَالْاَمْرُ ؕ تَبَارَكَ اللّٰهُ رَبُّ الْعٰلَمِيْنَ ۞

اُدْعُوْا رَبَّكُمْ تَضَرُّعًا وَّخُفْيَةً ؕ اِنَّهٗ لَا يُحِبُّ الْمُعْتَدِيْنَ ۞

وَلَا تُفْسِدُوْا فِى الْاَرْضِ بَعْدَ اِصْلَاحِهَا وَادْعُوْهُ خَوْفًا وَّطَمَعًا ؕ اِنَّ رَحْمَتَ اللّٰهِ قَرِيْبٌ مِّنَ الْمُحْسِنِيْنَ ۞

Surely your Lord is Allah, Who created the heavens and the earth in Six Days, then established Himself on the
Throne (of high Authority) befitting His Supreme Majesty.
He covers the night and the day by each other following swiftly; and (He created) the sun and the moon and the stars, all subservient to His Command. Listen!
His is the Creation and His is the Command.
Blessed is Allah, the Lord and Cherisher of all the Worlds!
Call on your Lord in all humility and in secrecy and surely Allah loves not these who trespass limits.

And do not make mischief in the earth after it has been set right and call on Him fearing and hoping (in your heart of hearts). Surely the Mercy of Allah is nigh to the doers of good.

Al A'raf 54,56

Significance: With the recital of the above verses, snakes and scorpions will not be able to harm — Insha Allah.

TO PREVENT DANGEROUS ANIMALS, HARMFUL INSECTS AND REPTILES FROM ENTERING THE HOUSE

A. اِنِّىْ تَوَكَّلْتُ عَلَى اللّٰهِ رَبِّىْ وَرَبِّكُمْ ۚ مَا مِنْ دَآبَّةٍ اِلَّا هُوَ اٰخِذٌۢ بِنَاصِيَتِهَا اِنَّ رَبِّىْ عَلٰى صِرَاطٍ مُّسْتَقِيْمٍ ۞

*Indeed, I rely in Allah, my Lord and your Lord.
There is no animal but He grasps it by its forelock. Surely, my Lord is on the Straight Path.*

Al Hud 56

Significance: Recite the above verse excessively — especially when going to bed and on awakening.

WHEN FEARING AN ATTACK FROM AN ANIMAL

A. اَللّٰهُ رَبُّنَا وَرَبُّكُمْ ۚ لَنَاۤ اَعْمٰلُنَا وَلَكُمْ اَعْمٰلُكُمْ ۚ لَا حُجَّةَ بَيْنَنَا وَبَيْنَكُمْ ۚ اَللّٰهُ يَجْمَعُ بَيْنَنَا ۚ

Allah is our Lord and your Lord.
For us is our deeds and for you, yours.
There is no argument between us and you.
Allah will bring us together.

Ash Shura 15

Significance: Read the above ayah and blow towards the animal. It won't attack — Insha Allah.

WHEN BITTEN BY A POISONOUS INSECT OR SNAKE

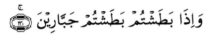

And when you grasp, you grasp like men with absolute power.
Ash Shu'ara 130

Significance: Circulate the finger around the bitten area and recite the above verse seven times in one breath. The patient will recover shortly — Insha Allah.

WHEN STUNG BY AN INSECT

Significance: Recite Suratul Inshirah (30th Juz) and blow on the patient. The pain will subside shortly — Insha Allah.

GENERAL PROTECTION

The Protector

Significance: Recite the above name of Allah excessively. No harm will be caused to the reciter even if he sleeps in a place where wild animals abound.

TO DRIVE OUT ANTS FROM THE HOUSE

يَاَيُّهَا النَّمْلُ ادْخُلُوْا مَسٰكِنَكُمْ لَا يَحْطِمَنَّكُمْ سُلَيْمٰنُ وَجُنُوْدُهٗ وَهُمْ لَا يَشْعُرُوْنَ ۝

O ants, enter your dwellings (so) Sulaimaan and his army do not trample you without knowing it.

An Naml 18

Significance: Upon reciting this verse, they will disappear very shortly — Insha Allah.

TO DRIVE OUT MOSQUITOES, FLEAS, ETC

وَمَا لَنَا اَلَّا نَتَوَكَّلَ عَلَى اللهِ وَقَدْ هَدٰىنَا سُبُلَنَا ۗ وَلَنَصْبِرَنَّ عَلٰى مَآ اٰذَيْتُمُوْنَا ۗ وَعَلَى اللهِ فَلْيَتَوَكَّلِ الْمُتَوَكِّلُوْنَ ۞

How should we not put our trust in Allah when He has shown us our ways.
We will surely endure that hurt which you cause us.
And in Allah let the trusting put their trust.

Ibrahim 12

Significance: To drive out mosquitoes, fleas etc. from the house or bedroom recite the above verse numerous times, the night will pass without disturbance — Insha Allah.

RELEASE FROM IMPRISONMENT

رَبَّنَآ اَخْرِجْنَا مِنْ هٰذِهِ الْقَرْيَةِ الظَّالِمِ اَهْلُهَا ۚ وَّاجْعَلْ لَنَا مِنْ لَّدُنْكَ وَلِيًّا ۙ وَّاجْعَلْ لَّنَا مِنْ لَّدُنْكَ نَصِيْرًا ۞

Our Lord, take us out of this town whose people are oppressors and raise for us from yourself one who will protect us

and raise for us from yourself one who will help us.

An Nisa 75

Significance: *If a person is trapped in a country or town as a result of the country or town being under siege or due to any other reason such as curfew etc. he should recite the above verse excessively. He will soon find a way out — Insha Allah.*

A MUSLIM'S INVISIBLE ENEMIES AND THE WAY TO OVERCOME THEM:

Allah explained to Muslims that they have hidden enemies, who do their best to mislead Muslims to disrespect Allah in this worldly life and to his displeasure in the Hereafter. Allah also guided Muslims to the method of delivery from the evils of these unseen enemies. The first of these enemies is the accursed Satan, who stirs up and leads all other enemies of man. Satan was not only a foe to our forefather Adam and our great grandmother Eve, but he is an open enemy of Adam's progeny till the end of this wordly life. Satan strives hard to persuade people either to disbelief or to commit sins in order that they may accompany him in dwelling forever in Hell. Satan is an incorporeal spirit, able to instill evil in man and allure mischief to him as if it were a second nature to him.

Allah explained to us how to overcome Satan and his followers. When a Muslim is about to commit a sin, or when he is maddened with anger, he should say:

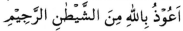

"I ask Allah for His refuge against the accursed Satan."

Then he should refrain himself from committing the sin and calm his anger. The Muslim should know that malicious incentives are always motivated by the Satan.

Allah said:

اِنَّ الشَّيْطٰنَ لَكُمْ عَدُوٌّ فَاتَّخِذُوْهُ عَدُوًّا ۚ اِنَّمَا يَدْعُوْا حِزْبَهٗ لِيَكُوْنُوْا مِنْ اَصْحٰبِ السَّعِيْرِ ۞

> "Surely, Satan is an enemy to you, so treat him as an enemy."

اللَّهُمَّ إِنِّي أَسْأَلُكَ يَا اللهُ بِأَنَّكَ الْوَاحِدُ الْأَحَدُ الصَّمَدُ الَّذِي لَمْ يَلِدْ وَلَمْ يُولَدْ وَلَمْ يَكُنْ لَهُ كُفُواً أَحَدٌ، أَنْ تَغْفِرَ لِي ذُنُوبِي إِنَّكَ أَنْتَ الْغَفُورُ الرَّحِيمُ

Allāhumma innee as-aluka yā Allāhu bi annakal wāhidul ahadus-samad allaḏhī lam yalid wa lam yūlad wa lam yakul-lahū kufuwan-ahad, antaghfira lī ḏhunūbī innaka antal-ghafūrur-rahīm

> O Allah, I ask You. O Allah, You are the One, the Only, Self-Sufficient Master, Who was not begotten and begets not and none is equal to Him. Forgive me my sins, surely you are Forgiving, Merciful.

اللَّهُمَّ إِنِّي ظَلَمْتُ نَفْسِي ظُلْماً كَثِيراً، وَلَا يَغْفِرُ الذُّنُوبَ إِلَّا أَنْتَ، فَاغْفِرْ لِي مَغْفِرَةً مِنْ عِنْدِكَ وَارْحَمْنِي إِنَّكَ أَنْتَ الْغَفُورُ الرَّحِيمُ

Allāhumma innee ḏhalamtu nafsi ḏhulman katheerā wa lā yaghfiruḏh-ḏhunūba illā anta, faghfirlī maghfiratan min 'indika warhamnī innaka antal ghafūrur-rahīm

> O Allah, I have greatly wronged myself and no one forgives sins but You. So grant me forgiveness, forgiveness from You, and have mercy on me. Surely, You are Forgiving, Merciful. [Bukhari & Muslim]

رَبَّنَا لَا تُزِغْ قُلُوبَنَا بَعْدَ إِذْ هَدَيْتَنَا وَهَبْ لَنَا مِنْ لَدُنْكَ رَحْمَةً إِنَّكَ أَنْتَ الْوَهَّابُ

Rabbanā lā tuzigh quloobanā ba'da idh hadaitanā wa hab lanā milladunka rahmah innaka antal-Wahhāb

> [Who say], "Our Lord, let not our hearts deviate after You have guided us and grant us from Yourself mercy. Indeed, You are the Bestower." [3:8]

www.ingramcontent.com/pod-product-compliance
Lightning Source LLC
LaVergne TN
LVHW011818240225
804421LV00004B/575